Take the Day ff

STUDY GUIDE

Take the Day Off

STUDY GUIDE

RECEIVING GOD'S GIFT OF REST

ROBERT MORRIS

Faith
Words

NEW YORK   NASHVILLE

FaithWords
Hachette Book Group
1290 Avenue of the Americas, New York, NY 10104
faithwords.com
twitter.com/faithwords

First Edition: January 2020

FaithWords is a division of Hachette Book Group, Inc.
The FaithWords name and logo are trademarks of Hachette Book Group, Inc.

The publisher is not responsible for websites (or their content) that are not owned by the publisher.

The Hachette Speakers Bureau provides a wide range of authors for speaking events.
To find out more, go to www.hachettespeakersbureau.com or call (866) 376-6591.

ISBN: 978-1-5460-1013-5

Printed in the United States of America

LSC-C

10 9 8 7 6 5 4 3 2 1

CONTENTS

INTRODUCTION

We serve an amazing God who, according to Philippians 4:19, "shall supply all your need according to His riches in glory by Christ Jesus." His name—Jehovah Jireh—means "the Lord will provide."

My first book, *The Blessed Life*, and my recent sequel, *Beyond Blessed*, explore the principle that God generously provides all the financial resources we need, and how we, as His children and bearers of His image, should be generous givers, too. While generosity is vitally important to experience the fullness of God's blessings, we must also understand how to wisely manage, or steward, our financial resources.

Take the Day Off deals with a different but equally vital principle—time. Just as we are to be good stewards and properly manage the financial blessings God provides, we are also called to wisely steward this gift of God.

During my early years as the founder and senior pastor of Gateway Church, I experienced a powerful example of the consequences of failing to heed the vital principle of rest that God gave His people in the fourth Commandment. This experience and the lessons learned in the years since have prompted me to share God's message about the Sabbath.

Remembering the Sabbath is a commandment God gave us. It's so important that, under the law of Moses, disobeying it was one of the handful of things that justified the death penalty. But it's also an eternal principle that speaks to how an individual relates to God, self, and creation.

The Sabbath was established at creation and played a fundamental role in enabling Israel to remain a distinct people and a healthy society throughout the centuries. It was God's plan for bringing the Savior of the world to the earth.

Take the Day Off explores the marvelous blessings that come from obeying the principle of Sabbath, as well as the disastrous consequences that come from failure to obey.

The world already suffers from an epidemic of stress, disease, and mental health problems that can clearly be traced back to our obsession with being busy and the effects of living life without margin. But the problem is not just lack of time, nor is it time management: it's a matter of the heart. Failure to obey the principle of Sabbath has eternal implications for the souls of men.

Once we understand that the gift of Sabbath is just that—a gift—we can learn how to relate to God in a way that will enable us to enter into His *eternal* rest. We will then also be examples to help bring others into that same relationship.

This study guide will lead you through each chapter of the book, expanding and presenting related material on some concepts and challenging your thinking with questions and exercises. It will tie together the Bible's examples of the principle of Sabbath with real-life modern-day stories and people. It will help you apply scriptural instruction and principles, along with current information and literature, to the vital issue of obeying God's commandment of Sabbath rest.

You can use this study guide for individual study or as a guide for discussion and teaching within your family or in small groups.

It was hard for me to learn to apply the principle of Sabbath, and it takes continuous effort—in the form of prayer, study, and worship—to maintain my level of stewardship. It will take effort on your part as well as self-evaluation to learn how to steward your time wisely. You will have to make choices, and some of those choices will be difficult ones.

As you implement and share the principle of Sabbath, you will encounter many enemies. The world is full of distractions. The culture doesn't want you to rest. The enemy of your soul doesn't want you to rest. Often your own soul won't want you to rest.

Thank God you have a Helper and a Guide to assist you in making those decisions and battling those enemies. You'll learn that rest helps fill the spiritual, physical, mental, and emotional tanks that fuel your life. Likewise, the Holy Spirit works in you through the emotions, sights, sounds, and experiences of life to help build your faith and trust in God. Remember, the Holy Spirit is a friend—not just a force.

God will bless, help, and reward your heartfelt efforts to be a better steward of your time and obey the principle of Sabbath. I pray that the Holy Spirit provides you the insight, emotions, images, and experiences that will enable you to *take the day off*.

CHAPTER ONE

THE FORGOTTEN COMMANDMENT

In order to properly perceive the significance of what may be the best known and most important direct encounter between God and the nation of Israel, it helps to understand the historical and prophetic context in which these events took place.

After having been enslaved in Egypt for generations, this multitude of people—perhaps two million—had been led to a place to wait for instructions. Just fifty days had elapsed since they left, and they had seen their God work incredible miracles, most notably the parting of the Red Sea and the destruction of the army of their former captors. They had been miraculously led out of bondage. But why? For what purpose?

The Israelites waited at the bottom of Mount Sinai for Moses to report back from his trip up to the top of the mountain. What happened on that summit would plot the course of history for generations to come.

This was not some wilderness camping trip. In fact, Moses had already explained to the people the gravity of this occasion and its main purpose.

Read Exodus 19:3–6. What did God tell Moses to say to the people about the reason for what was about to happen? What promises did God make to the Israelites in this passage?

_____

_____

_____

_____

In verse 7 we read that Moses "called for the elders of the people, and laid before them all these words which the LORD commanded them."

What was the response of the people in verse 8?

_____

_____

_____

_____

God then had Moses consecrate the people and warn them solemnly not to go up to the mountain or touch its base. Under threat of death, they were not to approach the mountain until they heard the long trumpet on the third day (v. 13). Verses 16–19 tell us what the nation of Israel saw and heard on that day:

> Then it came to pass on the third day, in the morning, that there were thunderings and lightnings, and a thick cloud on the mountain; and the sound of the trumpet was very loud, so that all the people who were in the camp trembled. And Moses brought the people out of the camp to meet with God, and they stood at the foot of the mountain. Now Mount Sinai was completely in smoke, because the Lord descended upon it in fire. Its smoke ascended like the smoke of a furnace, and the whole mountain quaked greatly. And when the blast of the trumpet sounded long and became louder and louder, Moses spoke, and God answered him by voice.

It says the people trembled at the sound of the trumpet. How do you think the Israelites felt when they heard and saw this? Why would they "tremble"?

_____

_____

_____

_____

God calls Moses back up to meet with Him, and then God sends him back down to warn the people again not to break through to come up the mountain (see v. 24).

Have you seen the movie *The Ten Commandments*?[1] In this film, the people wait and first hear the Ten Commandments when Moses brings the tablets down the mountain. However, that is not an accurate depiction of what happened.

Read Deuteronomy 4:9–13 and 32–36. What did the people see and hear that day? According to verse 35, why did God show Israel all these signs and wonders and prepare this covenant for them?

_____

_____

_____

_____

This was not the first covenant that God had created for His people. He had, in fact, spoken covenants with Adam, Noah, and Abraham. However, this covenant was different. The purpose of this Mosaic covenant was to set the Jewish people apart. They were to be the chosen people of all the earth. They would be the carriers of a special seed.

What does it mean that they were to be a "chosen" people? What seed were they carrying?

_____

_____

_____

_____

How does this seed relate both to the past and the future of the Israelites at that time? Specifically, how did it relate to the story of Adam and Eve and God's promise to Abraham (see Genesis 3:15)?

_____

_____

_____

_____

Moses returns from the mountain carrying two stone tablets. These represented the sacred written contract between God and the Israelites: There was one copy for each party to the covenant. These tablets contained ten stipulations, which the Bible calls the Ten Commandments. God deemed these standards of behavior and worship necessary for His people to abide by so that they could achieve the purpose and destiny for which He had chosen them.

The people had just heard God speak the Ten Commandments as they stood at the base of Mount Sinai. That experience was obviously quite impressive and memorable. Why do you think God thought it necessary to provide them with His commands in writing?

_____

_____

_____

_____

God's purpose in creating this covenant was to form a group of people who could remain distinct, intact, and healthy and who could thrive for centuries in a fallen, twisted, decaying world. Those Commandments were divinely designed to help them do just that. They were the heart of a system—along with the Levitical regulations found in Moses's books of Leviticus and Deuteronomy—that would create a unique culture and society. One that could resist being corrupted by the devastating effects of idolatry. One that could keep families intact, bodies and minds healthy, the land productive, and the social fabric strong. They are a remarkable set of rules for living.

Here in Exodus 20:1–17 is the text of these commands:

> God spoke all these words, saying:
>
> "I am the Lord your God, who brought you out of the land of Egypt, out of the house of bondage.
>
> "You shall have no other gods before Me.
>
> "You shall not make for yourself a carved image—any likeness of anything that is in heaven above, or that is in the earth beneath, or that is in the water under the earth; you shall not bow down to them nor serve them. For I, the Lord your God, am a jealous God, visiting the iniquity of the fathers upon the children to the third and fourth generations of those who hate Me, but showing mercy to thousands, to those who love Me and keep My commandments.

"You shall not take the name of the Lord your God in vain, for the Lord will not hold him guiltless who takes His name in vain.

"Remember the Sabbath day, to keep it holy. Six days you shall labor and do all your work, but the seventh day is the Sabbath of the Lord your God. In it you shall do no work: you, nor your son, nor your daughter, nor your male servant, nor your female servant, nor your cattle, nor your stranger who is within your gates. For in six days the Lord made the heavens and the earth, the sea, and all that is in them, and rested the seventh day. Therefore the Lord blessed the Sabbath day and hallowed it. [Bold added.]

"Honor your father and your mother, that your days may be long upon the land which the Lord your God is giving you.

"You shall not murder.

"You shall not commit adultery.

"You shall not steal.

"You shall not bear false witness against your neighbor.

"You shall not covet your neighbor's house; you shall not covet your neighbor's wife, nor his male servant, nor his female servant, nor his ox, nor his donkey, nor anything that is your neighbor's."

I have highlighted the fourth Commandment to make it easier to refer to later.

To what relationships do the first three Commandments refer?

_____

_____

_____

_____

To what relationships do the final six Commandments refer?

_____

_____

_____

_____

God didn't want the people to misunderstand what remembering and keeping the Sabbath looked like, so He followed the simple command with more explanation than He did any of the other ones.

We read in Exodus 31:14–15 that God took the fourth Commandment seriously: It was important enough to warrant the death penalty!

But did God really intend this to be enforced? Was He truly serious about making working on the Sabbath day a capital offense? Read Numbers 15:32–36.

What was the work that the man was guilty of doing on the Sabbath day? To whom did the people bring the man for trial? What was the punishment? *Who personally rendered the verdict and punishment on the man?*

_____

_____

_____

_____

Notice that the whole community was to participate in the stoning of the guilty party. Why do you think God gave this specific command? Does this whole scene and these consequences seem harsh to you? Explain.

_____

_____

_____

_____

Keep in mind that the laws Moses delivered to the Israelites were designed for their benefit *and* to ensure the success of God's grand plan of redemption. The laws contained principles for remaining healthy as individuals and families and strong as a society. God understood what we clearly do not. Namely, that a society in which people work seven days a week is just as vulnerable to collapse as a society in which people are free to rape and murder without consequence. God was crafting a culture and a people who could survive and thrive so that in the fullness of time, His only begotten Son could enter the world through them.

A Rest Remains

There is a vital wisdom principle embedded in the fourth Commandment. I'm talking about the principle of rest. This principle is a thread that runs throughout the Bible.

The book of Hebrews is a New Testament book devoted almost completely to explaining how the New Covenant relates to the Old. In the fourth chapter there is an entire passage that addresses the principle of rest. It begins in verses 3–5 (NLT):

> So God's rest is there for people to enter, but those who first heard this good news failed to enter because they disobeyed God. So God set another time for entering his rest, and that time is today. God announced this through David much later in the words already quoted: "Today when you hear his voice, don't harden your hearts." Now if Joshua had succeeded in giving them this rest, God would not have spoken about another day of rest still to come. So there is a special rest still waiting for the people of God.

If a Sabbath rest is "still waiting for the people of God," or as the New King James Version says, "There remains a Sabbath rest for the people of God," what does that mean for you and me today?

_____

_____

_____

_____

Read also Hebrews 3:19. According to these passages, what kind of act is this? Why did God "set another time for entering His rest"?

_____

_____

_____

_____

The Israelites had refused to take possession of the land where they could rest as a nation because of their lack of faith—their unbelief.

The fact is, the principle of rest is a pattern established right from the beginning of creation, and it's still in place today. As we've seen, God personally inscribed it into the Ten Commandments. We've also seen that it is revalidated in the New Testament. And although as a pastor I was familiar with the principle, its importance and relevance had not been fully clear to me until I hit that wall of exhaustion I described at the beginning of the book. With the best of intentions, I had allowed my love for people and the demands of leading a church to progressively crowd out any space for real rest in my life. Because I was chronically ignoring the principle of the Sabbath, I couldn't participate in God's divine plan of restoration.

Sadly, many people ignore the Old Testament and think it no longer applies to Christians. Let's examine this assumption.

Law, Grace, and Principles

How New Covenant believers view and relate to the Old Covenant laws has been a point of contention since the Book of Acts. However, the very understanding that we have just explored *why* God gave the Old Covenant laws—namely, to create a separated, healthy, thriving people who could carry the seed of the Redeemer in this fallen world until His time to come forth finally arrived—gives us the key to understanding how to relate to those laws under the New Covenant.

Under the New Covenant, does keeping the Mosaic laws have anything to do with our salvation or standing with God? Why or why not?

_____

_____

_____

_____

The Old Covenant laws, especially the Ten Commandments, still reflect God's values, character, and wisdom for living. If they are no longer laws, however, what do they represent, and why should we heed them?

_____

_____

_____

_____

Wisdom is still wisdom, regardless of the age. Read Exodus 20:10–11 again. From what event and time did God model this principle?

_____

_____

_____

_____

I learned the hard way that there are benefits to observing the principles embedded in the Ten Commandments and there are consequences when we do not. Here's a quick exercise to help you clarify why this is so. Read each one of the ten and ask yourself two questions: "Are there benefits to incorporating this command into my life?" and "Are there negative consequences in life if I do not?" Write down some benefits and consequences for the following examples:

The first Commandment: "You shall have no other gods before Me."

_____

_____

_____

_____

The sixth Commandment: "You shall not murder."

_____

_____

_____

_____

The eighth commandment: "You shall not bear false witness against your neighbor."

_____

_____

_____

_____

We affirm these and other commands without hesitation because we clearly understand that violating them will do harm to ourselves, others, our community, or all three. What's the general term for these things that God wants to keep us from?

_____

Why do we seem to exempt the fourth Commandment from the logic that God gave us these principles to protect us?

_____

_____

_____

_____

How does keeping these commandments relate to our salvation by grace through Jesus Christ?

_____

_____

_____

_____

"The wisdom contained in the Old Testament laws didn't suddenly stop being wisdom the weekend Jesus died on the cross and rose from the dead." What does this affirmation mean to you?

_____

_____

_____

_____

The miracle of the new birth does several extraordinary things inside each person who says yes to God's gracious offer of salvation in His Son. It makes a formerly dead spirit alive with the life of God. It cleanses the conscience. It imparts a spirit of adoption by which the heart begins to recognize that God is a person's loving Father. What additional *very important thing* does this miracle do?

_____

_____

_____

You, the believer, no longer need to refer to tablets of stone. The things that please God are encoded right into your inner being.

Rest Is a Step of Faith

As the author of Hebrews reminds us, honoring the principle of the Sabbath takes faith. What is the reaction that most Christians have to the idea of unplugging for a full day each week? What is your immediate reaction to the idea?

_____

_____

_____

How are people's reaction to the teachings about Sabbath similar to their reaction to the teachings about tithing? How does the principle of tithing and the benefits of it relate to the principle and benefits of Sabbath rest? In each case, why do we need to put our trust in God?

_____

_____

_____

Read Hebrews 4:11 in the Amplified Version:

Let us therefore be zealous and exert ourselves and strive diligently to enter that rest [of God, to know and experience it for ourselves], that no one may fall or perish by the same kind of unbelief and disobedience [into which those in the wilderness fell].

Why is diligence required to enter into the Sabbath rest that is so important to God?

_____

_____

_____

A number of years ago, when I was on the pastoral staff of another church prior to starting Gateway Church, I had an encounter with a pastor friend over lunch. The Lord tried to get through to me that day about the importance of a regular weekly Sabbath rest. Of course, I didn't heed His warning at that time, and it was several years later when I hit the wall over my lack of socks and underwear.

Have you ever experienced a time when the Lord was trying to teach you something and you just didn't get it, only to learn the lesson the hard way later in life? Explain.

_____

_____

_____

_____

Rest: Better Late than Never

For the tribes of Israel, Saturday was their only option for a day of rest. God had very explicitly commanded that the seventh day of the week be set aside for rest because He rested from His creative labors after the sixth day. Under the New Covenant, however, we are not attempting to keep the letter of the law. Paul explains in Romans 7 that the law was given to show mankind that we are sinful and in need of a Redeemer. We are honoring the eternal principles contained in God's commandments while continuing to stand in Jesus' finished work on the cross for our righteousness and right standing with God.

The Pharisees harshly criticized Jesus for healing on the Sabbath. They'd lost sight of the *spirit* of the law and were hung up on being sticklers about the *letter* of the law.

Read Matthew 5:27–28. How does Jesus expand upon the spirit of the law as opposed to the letter of the law in this passage?

_____

_____

_____

The principle of the Sabbath is to set aside and protect one day out of seven and devote it to rest and fellowship with God. In the New Covenant era, it isn't essential for this special day to be Saturday. Any day is fine.

Decades ahead of me, my pastor friend had discovered a major key to not only surviving but also actually thriving. The principle is simply that one day in seven is to be set aside and jealously protected.

My weekly day is Monday. It took some time and effort to explain and demonstrate to people that I was serious about this Sabbath principle, and for a good reason. Eventually, I received fewer invitations to Monday meetings.

I related the story of a member of my staff who invited me to a Monday meeting because "it was for a good cause." I pretended to be offended and asked if it was okay to break any commandment if "it was for a good cause."

Have you ever struggled with a decision that would break a commandment because it seemed like the result would be a good thing? Explain.

_____

_____

_____

Before I took eight weeks off (six weeks' paid sabbatical and two weeks' vacation), I had been pushing myself to the limits. During my time off, God showed me that I needed to recoup my fifty-two days of rest for the entire year.

Read Leviticus 25:2–5. What does this passage teach about how God applies the principle of Sabbath to other parts of His creation? How do farmers apply this principle to the land in modern times?

_____

_____

_____

Read 2 Chronicles 36:19–21. How long did the people of Israel neglect the land's Sabbath? How long were they in exile?

_____

_____

_____

Describe in your own words what it means in verse 21 of the New Living Translation when it says, "The land finally enjoyed its Sabbath rest."

_____

_____

_____

For whom has God designed the Sabbath?

_____

_____

_____

_____

Read Matthew 11:28–30. At this moment in your life, do you feel burdened and heavy-laden? Could you use more rest for your soul? Explain.

_____

_____

_____

_____

Key Quotes:

"The eternal fate of humanity itself hinged on the Israelites' ability to remain a distinct people and a healthy, successful society through the centuries."

"Those ten simple covenant stipulations, carved onto those stone tablets by God's own finger, are a truly remarkable set of rules for living."

"A society in which people work seven days a week is just as vulnerable to collapse as a society in which people are free to rape and murder without consequence."

"The principle of rest is a pattern established right from the beginning of creation and it is still in place today."

"Wisdom is still wisdom—even if law keeping is no longer the pathway to a relationship with God."

"I had to come to the realization that honoring the Sabbath is on the same list as not killing people."

"If you don't learn to honor this principle, the day will come when you no longer have a choice but to stop and rest."

CHAPTER TWO

WHO HAS TIME TO REST?

In Japan they call it *karōshi*. The Chinese have their own word for it: *guolaosi*. And in South Korea they call it *gwarosa*. All three terms were coined fairly recently to describe something so new that their languages didn't have a word for it. These words describe the act of literally working yourself to death. All three of these cultures discovered they needed a word to describe an increasingly common phenomenon: people dropping dead at their jobs as a result of working insane hours, under intense pressure, with little to no rest.

This has been a more common phenomenon in Asia, which does not have the Christian biblical foundation on which most of Western civilization was built. Resting one day a week is part of that. (Even the government of South Korea, however, has recently become more aware and proactive about this problem. In 2018 their parliament passed a bill reducing the maximum workweek from sixty-eight hours to fifty-two hours.)[1]

Why do you think someone would routinely work over a hundred hours per week?

_____

_____

_____

_____

While our culture's biblical foundation has been under attack for decades, it still contains enough remnants of our Christian values and ethics to provide at least some residual respect for the Sabbath in our culture. Forty years ago, most stores in America were closed on Sunday. In 2019, there remain just a handful of states, such as New Jersey and North Dakota, that have retained some form of what are known as "blue laws," restricting Sunday trading, typically for alcohol and car sales.

Otherwise, Christian-owned companies, such as Chick-fil-A and Hobby Lobby, are about the only businesses routinely closed on Sundays anymore.

How do you feel about stores or businesses being required to close on Sundays?

_____

_____

_____

The overworking in Asian societies, in particular in Japan, has also resulted in a phenomenon of increased suicides. For increasing numbers of overworked people in these cultures, suicide seems to be the only pathway to rest.

Americans don't typically work sixteen hours a day, seven days per week at one job. In Massachusetts they could not do so anyway, as that state still has a "Sabbath" type law on their books: "Most employers must allow a worker to have one day off after 6 consecutive days of work. This day off must include an unbroken period between 8 a.m. and 5 p.m."[2]

For Americans, it is more about allowing ourselves to be pulled in a dozen different directions, all the time, every day. We may have multiple jobs. We have demanding full-time jobs plus countless other things vying for attention. We're chronically, unendingly, terminally busy.

How many hours do you or members of your immediate family spend each week at their regular job or jobs?

_____

_____

_____

Many Americans are addicted to work, and the term *workaholic* is not necessarily viewed in a negative way. In fact, busyness is often viewed as something of a status symbol.

However, too much work and busyness takes a toll on us. As the British proverb says, "All work and no play makes Jack a dull boy." (And that proverb was first used as early as the 1600s.)

Do you feel like you are being lazy or unproductive if you aren't working or busy? Why or why not?

_____

_____

_____

_____

Too Much of a Good Thing

There is, of course, nothing wrong with hard work. Quite the contrary. The Book of Proverbs warns many times against being idle or lazy. And in Exodus 20:9, God's commandment about the Sabbath includes the command, "Six days you shall labor and do all your work." God's direct command to rest one day out of seven is built upon the assumption that you're going to put in six good, vigorous days of work in your vocation and around your home. Up until the twentieth century, most work consisted of six days tending to a farm or homestead.

What stories can you remember, either from your own family's past, stories from friends, or even what you have read in books, about rural life in America prior to the growth of the industrial revolution? Do you view that way of life critically or do you view it fondly, with a sense of nostalgia? Explain.

_____

_____

_____

_____

Today, most of us work five-day-a-week jobs. For many, those jobs involve a lengthy commute to and from the workplace. It's not unusual for someone to leave the house before sunrise and not return until the sun has set. We then attempt to attend to everything related to house, yard, and family on the nights and weekends. Around all of this we cram in events, obligations, clubs, second jobs, and, for parents with kids at home, their endless school projects and extra-curricular activities.

A previous question asked how much time you or your family members spent at your job. Now, let's consider this question: How much time do you or immediate family members spend at the obligations mentioned above?

_____

_____

_____

_____

The Internet and social media platforms also vie for our attention. One recent study shows that the average person spends two hours and twenty-two minutes per day on social media.[3] For young people age sixteen to twenty-four, that time is in excess of three hours per day.

That amount of time is significant, but so is the fact that much of the time the vast majority of our social media feeds and news feeds represent an unending stream of bad news, atrocity, and catastrophe.

Other social media platforms are more about making you feel inadequate, unlovely, uncool, or boring. They create the illusion that everyone you know is living a better life than you.

How much time do you typically spend on social media? What sites or types of information do you spend time on? How does spending time on social media affect you?

_____

_____

_____

_____

For most of us, our phones are in reach twenty-four hours a day, seven days a week. We know the dangers of texting while driving, and some jurisdictions now prohibit a driver from even holding a phone in their hand while driving, yet we still use them while driving in our cars.

Yes, we've essentially hooked ourselves up to a constant IV drip of worry, outrage, fear, and negativity inserted directly into our already-weary souls.

How often do you use your cell phone, and for what purposes? Do you think there should be more or fewer restrictions on cell phone use? Explain.

_____

_____

_____

_____

Hard work is important. But consistent hard work is only sustainable if we honor another of God's immutable, unchangeable principles. The principle of rest.

Noble Motives, Out of Balance

Why don't we rest more often? Many times, a noble sense of responsibility drives us to work as much as we possibly can. After all, 1 Timothy 5:8 says, "But if anyone does not provide for his own, and especially for those of his household, he has denied the faith and is worse than an unbeliever."

Worse than an unbeliever! No Christian would want to be guilty of such a sin. So it is easy to rationalize ignoring God's command to rest one day out of seven. However, providing and resting are both commands of God. So is "Do not steal." He wouldn't want us to disobey one command in order to obey the other.

To rest is a step of faith. To what other command of God is this step of faith comparable? Explain.

_____

_____

_____

_____

When you take a day each week to rest, it requires you to trust God to supernaturally help you fulfill all your responsibilities in the six remaining days. You also have to trust that God will supernaturally bless the 90 percent of your income that remains after you tithe the first 10 percent.

Learning to rest actually helps you fulfill your responsibilities. By giving both your body and your soul rest, you become more effective and efficient at everything you do the other six days of the week.

Explain in your own words Stephen Covey's concept of "sharpening the saw" and the point of Abraham Lincoln's quote about sharpening the axe.

_____

_____

_____

_____

Explain how the Sabbath as a day of rest and celebration distinguished the nation of Israel from the rest of the ancient world.

_____

_____

_____

_____

Was getting weekly rest any easier in ancient times than it is today? Explain.

_____

_____

_____

_____

Redeeming Rest

Read Hebrews 3:18–4:2 in the Amplified Version.

What, according to this passage in Hebrews, prevents us from entering God's rest? What is the only alternative to trusting in God? How did this affect the Israelites entering the land God had promised them?

_____

_____

_____

_____

Describe how you think the trials Israel endured and the way God provided for them should have led them to trust Him.

_____

_____

_____

_____

Describe what the prophet meant in Isaiah 30:15–16: "For thus the Lord God, the Holy One of Israel, has said, 'In repentance and rest you will be saved, in quietness and trust is your strength.' But you were not willing" (NASB).

_____

_____

_____

_____

How are we today often unwilling to accept God's rest?

_____

_____

_____

_____

Redeeming Work

God assumes that the remaining six days revolve around work.

Our waking moments are largely filled with talking about work, thinking about work, planning for work, looking forward to work, or dreading work. We feel guilty if we don't do enough of it, or we feel resentful when we work too much. Our lives revolve around work, but often it's not the actual work that exhausts us. It's the worry, fretting, stress, and anxiety about it that wears us out.

The truth is, work—that is, meaningful, productive things to do that bear fruit—is a divine gift of God.

Read Genesis 2:15 and 3:17–19.

When did God give mankind work? Why did God give mankind work? How is the gift of work related to the curse of the ground—the "toil" mentioned in 3:17 or the "sweat" in 3:19?

_____

_____

_____

_____

How do you feel about work in general? Does your work currently exhaust you or fulfill you? Do you look forward to work or dread it? Write down an example of both.

_____

_____

_____

_____

If you feel like work is dreaded drudgery, what are two possible things this could indicate?

_____

_____

_____

_____

Read Galatians 3:13. Jesus Christ has redeemed us from the curse. For the born-again believer, Jesus has provided a way to view work that rises above the sweat and toil of this world. Just as you've been redeemed by the work of Jesus on the cross, your work has been redeemed as well!

In what ways is the Hebrew term *avodah* translated? How is it translated in Exodus 8:1 in the New International Version?

_____

_____

_____

_____

Describe in your own words what it means that work can be a form of worship. How might that relate to our everyday lives based on Romans 12:1?

_____

_____

_____

_____

How can you begin to better see the sacred nature of work and its kingdom implications?

_____

_____

_____

_____

Write down at least a few things to thank God for regarding your work, whether it be a regular job for income or the work you do around your household or in your community.

_____

_____

_____

_____

Your work is your vocation. It is your _calling_ from God.

Describe the current separation of work from the concept of ministry. Is a pastor or missionary more involved in the work of the Lord than an accountant, schoolteacher, or homemaker? Explain.

_____

_____

_____

_____

Remember, whatever you do for a living as a child of God is _not_ secular. It's sacred.

Redeeming Time

Have you ever prayed to God for more time? What was the circumstance? What was the outcome?

_____

_____

_____

_____

What are the similarities between these two fallacies?: (1) It would help to have more time when we are under pressure. (2) It would help to have more money when we are under financial pressure.

_____

_____

_____

_____

Fill in the blank: Better _____ of time is the answer to lack of time.

We cannot "make time." Nor can we "save time." We constantly hear talk about time-saving devices and saving time through special techniques and short-cuts. We essentially talk about time much in the same way we do about money. Yet we really _can_ save money, but we can only spend, manage, and invest time. We can never save it.

_____

_____

_____

_____

My efforts at choosing the best driving lane or the shortest bank teller line invariably end up wrong. In what ways do you try to save time?

_____

_____

_____

_____

What was the result of my mind wandering to solve a problem back home when I was a guest minister at another church? How did God respond? What was the lesson I learned?

_____

_____

_____

The first time God introduced the Sabbath commandment, He explained it in terms of His six days of creation. He said, "For in six days the Lord made the heavens and the earth, the sea, and all that is in them, and rested the seventh day." In Deuteronomy 5:12–15, He explains the meaning of Sabbath in the context of the people having been slaves in Egypt.

In this example in Deuteronomy, of what does the Sabbath remind us?

_____

_____

_____

Consider the story I shared about MBA students and time management from Stephen Covey's book *First Things First*.[4] What is the lesson of this story from a time-management standpoint?

_____

_____

_____

What is the biggest of the "big rocks" where your time is concerned? Why?

_____

_____

_____

_____

Key Quotes:

"We're chronically, unendingly, terminally busy."

"Busyness is often more than a mere habit. For many it's actually an addiction."

"Work is not the enemy. The temptation to not rest is the enemy."

"The principle of the Sabbath is a gift! It is a weekly celebration, a party even."

"Rest is a gift from God but it requires faith to receive it."

"Our work can be a form of worship where we simultaneously honor the Lord through our excellence and diligence, serve our families by providing for them, and serve our communities by adding value."

"Whatever you do for a living as a child of God is *not* secular. It's sacred."

"We have to *schedule* and *protect* the most important things we want to accomplish. Otherwise, you'll never fit them in."

CHAPTER THREE

THE FOUR TANKS

Anyone who lives in Texas is familiar with the vast number of eighteen-wheeler tanker trucks that crisscross this vast state.

One day, the Lord used one of those tanker trucks as an analogy to burn into my heart an unforgettable message about my calling as a pastor and a teacher. He said, "Robert, you are a fuel truck. That is your job." Immediately, I envisioned one of those familiar eighteen-wheelers. The Lord continued: "Your job involves going from station to station to fill up their tanks with the fuel from your truck." I knew immediately what He meant. I have to fill up my family. I have to fill up the elders of our church, the staff, the lay-leadership, and, of course, the membership. It occurred to me that I even supply pastors from other churches because Gateway has grown to be a place where many churches around the country look for advice and encouragement.

It made sense to me. My job is to refuel other people. But the moment I made the connection of that analogy, I had another realization. The gasoline tanker truck called "Robert Morris" was nearly empty most of the time! I knew I was ministering to everyone with a tank that was nearly dry, and in that moment, God called me out on it. But for some time, misplaced guilt hampered my ability to truly take a day of rest.

Describe a time when you knew there was something very important to do, but you were unable to find the time or other resources because of something you considered more urgent at the time.

_____

_____

_____

_____

Early on after making a decision to take a day of rest, I tried to take Monday off. However, most of the church staff and other people I knew were at work that day. A combination of religious obligation and manly pride worked together to convince me I was doing something wrong by not doing something productive, even though I had just finished a draining weekend of work.

It started small, with just a peek at an email or two, but it escalated relentlessly. Lacking clear boundaries and strong conviction about the principle of Sabbath, the inappropriate guilt I felt about doing nothing led me to work on Mondays. Not only that, but even when I didn't work much, the guilty mindset stole my peace. I was killing myself with work until the Lord likened me to a fuel truck that had no fuel left to share with others.

Describe a time when you were struggling to go down a certain path or trying to accomplish something and you were finally "brought back to reality" about the situation.

_____

_____

_____

_____

I thought the Lord wanted me to be able to minister to others from a tank that was nearly full. Once again, the Lord corrected me.

Read Psalm 23:5. Describe the shift in paradigm I described as the miracle of the Sabbath in this encounter.

_____

_____

_____

_____

Your Four Tanks

As we noted earlier, every believer is a minister as much as a pastor or a church leader. Likewise, regardless of what you do for a living, you need fuel to share with all your relationships. There are people who depend on you in a wide variety of ways.

Read Matthew 5:13–16. What metaphors does Jesus use to describe believers in this passage? How does the concept of replenishing resources (filling the tank) apply to these metaphors?

_____

_____

_____

I had allowed myself to feel guilty about the little bit of downtime that was absolutely essential to my ability to continue to supply others.

What are the four reservoirs of our lives that we must regularly refuel to ensure we're overflowing for others?

_____

_____

_____

I described the phone call I had during my early ministry at Gateway with a friend of mine who helped me apply these four tank principles and help my friend in the process. What was my recommendation to him?

_____

_____

_____

You will be amazed how good you will feel when you find the things that replenish your four tanks.

Your Spiritual Tank

Spending time praying and reading God's Word is the best way to fill your spiritual tank. Unfortunately, many believers view these life-giving activities as more of an obligatory chore than a nourishing, refreshing privilege.

What are some things you were brought up with that you "ought" to do that you found unpleasant? Do you still feel as though even things that are good for you are unpleasant if they are presented as obligations? Explain.

_____

_____

_____

_____

For whose benefit is the Sabbath rest?

_____

_____

_____

_____

The fact is, taking time to be alone and still with God isn't a gift to Him. It's a gift to yourself—a very necessary gift. Why is this statement true?

_____

_____

_____

_____

According to Ephesians 6:10–12, with what or whom do we do battle every day as Christians?

_____

_____

_____

_____

In 2 Timothy 2:1, the apostle Paul exhorted Timothy to "*be strong* in the grace that is in Christ Jesus" (emphasis added). I also encourage you to be strong spiritually as Paul exhorts in Ephesians 3:16. In other words, keep your spiritual tank overflowing.

In addition to prayer and spending time in the Word, what are some other things you can do to help fill your spiritual tank?

_____

_____

_____

_____

Your Physical Tank

What are the two basic pillars of physical fitness that are regularly promoted?

_____

_____

_____

According to the book by Saundra Dalton-Smith, what are some of the warning indicators of a "physical rest deficit"?[1]

_____

_____

_____

To what negative health effects has chronically bad sleep been related?

_____

_____

_____

Rest in the form of sleep is clearly vital, but there are also certain forms of physical activity that tend to restore you rather than deplete you physically. Those activities will differ from person to person.

What kind of physical activity might help restore rather than deplete *you*? If you don't know, what do you think you might want to try?

_____

_____

_____

_____

Your Emotional Tank

We all have an emotional tank that can run dry. When it does, we feel numb. We're irritable and find it difficult to handle stressful situations. We tend to find it difficult or impossible to generate enthusiasm, even for things we've enjoyed in the past. We struggle to focus on vital tasks.

The primary fuel for your emotional tank is something the Bible calls *joy*. It's no accident that Psalm 28:7 associates divine joy with strength.

Joy is also a fruit of the Spirit (see Galatians 5:22).

John 16:24 says that when you ask something in Jesus' name, you will receive, and your *joy* will be full.

A *joyful* heart is good medicine according to Proverbs 17:22 (ESV).

What do these other Scriptures say about joy? Romans 15:13; James 1:2; Psalm 16:11; Psalm 118:24.

_____

_____

_____

_____

What did C. S. Lewis call joy?

_____

_____

_____

_____

The famous early-twentieth-century evangelist Billy Sunday once noted, "If you have no joy, there's a leak in your Christianity somewhere." That leak is in your emotional tank. Or put another way, you're not engaging in the kinds of restful activities that replenish and refill it.

For me, the primary restful activities that fill and refresh me emotionally involve being around family and friends.

What kind of restful activities refresh you emotionally? If nothing comes to mind, what might you try?

_____

_____

_____

_____

Your Mental Tank

God created the human mind with an enormous capacity. When healthy, our brains can process amazing amounts of information, synthesize it, draw conclusions from it, and retain it. You really are carrying a miracle of information management and processing between your ears. But like any other part of your body, soul, or spirit, it will only function as God designed it if you keep it healthy. Rest and restorative activity are the keys to that health.

Reading is a large part of filling my mental tank. Not every book I read has to do with spiritual things, theology, pastoring, or leadership. I used to feel guilty if I wasn't reading material related to my duties as a pastor. In reality, when I was reading work-related content at home on my day off, I was basically *working* as opposed to resting. My mind was applying what I was reading to my work life. That was draining, rather than refilling, my mental tank. I now make it a point on my Sabbath days to read things that interest me—things that have no direct relationship to or impact on my workday responsibilities.

What kind of books or other materials do you like to read? Do you listen to audiobooks while you drive? Do you read to learn, enjoy, or a combination of the two? Explain.

_____

_____

_____

_____

_____

I also enjoy watching funny movies, as long as they don't contain inappropriate content.

Numerous studies reveal that healthy lifestyles can improve brain function as we age. In addition, there are a number of brain exercises you can do to help sharpen your mental skills:

1. Test your recall. Make a list—of grocery items, things to do, or anything else that comes to mind—and memorize it. An hour or so later, see how many items you can recall. Make items on the list as challenging as possible for the greatest mental stimulation.

2. Let the music play. Learn to play a musical instrument or join a choir. Studies show that learning something new and complex over a longer period of time is ideal for the aging mind.

3. Do math in your head. Figure out problems without the aid of pencil, paper, or computer; you can make this more difficult—and athletic—by walking at the same time.

4. Take a cooking class. Learn how to cook a new cuisine. Cooking uses a number of senses: smell, touch, sight, and taste, which all involve different parts of the brain.

5. Learn a foreign language. The listening and hearing involved stimulates the brain. What's more, a rich vocabulary has been linked to a reduced risk for cognitive decline.

6. Create word pictures. Visualize a word in your head; then try and think of any other words that begin (or end) with the same two letters.

7. Draw a map from memory. After returning home from visiting a new place, try to draw a map of the area; repeat this exercise each time you visit a new location.

8. Challenge your taste buds. When eating, try to identify individual ingredients in your meal, including subtle herbs and spices.

9. Refine your hand-eye abilities. Take up a new hobby that involves fine-motor skills, such as knitting, drawing, painting, assembling a puzzle, and so on.

10. Learn a new sport. Start doing an athletic exercise that utilizes both mind and body, such as yoga, golf, or tennis.[2]

What do you currently do to sharpen your mental skills? Do any of these options sound interesting to you?

_____

_____

_____

_____

Monitor Your Fuel Levels

People don't seem to run out of fuel as much as when I was a young man. In small-town East Texas in the '70s, there wasn't a gas station on every corner like there is in our urban areas today.

The primary reason we don't is that our gas gauges today are much more sophisticated and accurate. While in the past "E" meant empty, you didn't really know how close you were to running out of gas. Today's cars can project the (nearly) precise number of miles you can drive before the tank is empty. Our cars are better at monitoring our fuel levels.

Have you ever run out of gas? Why and where did it happen?

_____

_____

_____

_____

Not talking about driving a car, what do you mean when you say you feel like you've "run out of gas"?

_____

_____

_____

When it comes to your four fuel tanks, no flashing "low fuel" light is going to illuminate on your forehead when you're dangerously low in any of these areas. All you have is your own willingness to monitor yourself, along with the Holy Spirit within you, of course. Jesus called Him "the Helper" for a reason. If you let Him, and have a spiritual ear inclined to His voice, He'll let you know. The problem is that when your spiritual tank is low, you're also likely to be spiritually hard of hearing. That's why the principle of Sabbath is so important.

It's essential to know what replenishes these four key areas of your life.

Which of the four areas is likely to be the most difficult for you to learn to replenish? Which is likely to be the easiest? Why?

_____

_____

_____

Right now, what recharges you spiritually?

_____

_____

_____

Mentally?

_____

_____

_____

Physically?

_____

_____

_____

Emotionally?

_____

_____

_____

Remember, the Sabbath isn't a religious chore you have to do so God won't be mad at you. It's a gift God has instructed you to give yourself so you can be His healthy, productive, long-lived representative to a broken world and accomplish everything He put you on this earth to do.

Key Quotes:

"I don't want you ministering from a tank that's merely *almost* full. I want you ministering from an *overflowing* tank."

"Simply setting aside one day in seven to recharge and reconnect with God is the key to living in overflow mode."

"We must regularly refuel all four tanks to make sure we are overflowing for others."

"Spending time praying and reading God's Word is the best way to fill your spiritual tank."

"There is simply no way to recharge your physical tank without rest."

"The primary fuel for your emotional tank is something the Bible calls *joy*."

CHAPTER FOUR

THE SABBATH WAS MADE FOR YOU

Jewish families who want a modern kitchen but choose to strictly observe the Jewish dietary laws—that is, to "keep kosher"—have a daunting task before them.

At the heart of creating a kosher kitchen lies the need to meticulously keep all dairy products away from meat items. That requires owning two refrigerators. But that's not all. You also have to keep everything that touches meat away from everything that touches dairy. So duplicate sets of pots, pans, mixing bowls, and utensils have to not only be kept but also kept separate from one another and easily identified as to which side of the kitchen they belong. They must never get mixed up. This extends to having two dishwashers. Even after all the equipment and storage is in place, keeping kosher still requires strict attention to planning, scheduling, sequence, and process in food preparation to make sure meat and dairy never become part of the same meal.

What Scripture does this restriction about refraining from mixing meat and dairy come from?

_____

_____

_____

_____

Based on Leviticus 17:5–7, what is one possible explanation of the origin of this practice?

_____

_____

_____

_____

What are some of the other kosher dietary restrictions that grew directly out of that one command?

_____

_____

_____

_____

The *kashrut*, or kosher dietary laws, include much more than instructions about meat and dairy. If you are interested in more detailed information, see this online review from Kenyon College.[1]

In a word, what was the reason that the simple instruction not to boil a goat in its mother's milk became a complex and burdensome system of rules? In what other actions by Adam and Eve and the citizens of Babel did this impulse manifest itself?

_____

_____

_____

_____

How many commandments and instructions are contained in Exodus, Leviticus, Numbers, and Deuteronomy? To what level of rules had that grown by the time of Jesus? What was this complex oral rabbinical teaching called?

_____

_____

_____

_____

Based on the statements of Jesus in Matthew 15:6–9 and Luke 11:46, describe in your own words Jesus' condemnations of the religious leaders at the time.

_____

_____

_____

_____

Something very similar happened with God's commandment concerning the Sabbath. Over the centuries, many additional restrictions and wrinkles had been added to God's fairly straightforward command to rest on the seventh day. Jesus was always exasperating and infuriating the religious leaders of His day by refusing to abide by all of the extra provisions and restrictions that had been added through the centuries. Jesus recognized that they'd turned what God meant to be a blessing into a burdensome obligation.

As we see in the quote from Pastor Mark Buchanan's book *The Rest of God*,[2] standing between us and experiencing the power of the Sabbath principle are one obstacle and one pitfall. The **obstacle** is busyness. The **pitfall** is legalism.

Life, Not Law

The Gospel of Matthew records that Jesus was traveling and ministering in the towns and villages encircling the Sea of Galilee—the region where he'd grown from childhood into manhood. His message, however, fell largely on unhearing ears.

Read Matthew 11:20–25. Which cities (that He had just visited) does Jesus call out and warn about their hard-heartedness? How serious are these warnings? (Note the comparison in verse 24.)

_____

_____

_____

_____

Read verses 28–30. Based on this change to a gentle and pleading tone, what is the likely reason that the people there were unable to respond to the miracles and glory that Jesus displayed?

_____

_____

_____

Rest! It's no coincidence that the next few stories in Matthew's gospel center around Jesus and the Sabbath—God's designated day of rest for His people. Matthew 12 opens with Jesus and His disciples walking through a grain field on the Sabbath. As they walked, the obviously hungry group picked a few heads of ripe grain from the stalk and ate them. The Pharisees, the self-appointed law police, were apparently watching from a distance because they immediately pulled Jesus over and tried to write Him a citation.

Read Matthew 12:2–8. In addition to the fact that Jesus was teaching and criticizing the Pharisees, which Old Testament character did Jesus compare Himself to? In verses 6–8, what dramatic, powerful, and controversial point does He reveal to them?

_____

_____

_____

_____

What specific language indicated these clear pronouncements? What was the reaction of the Pharisees?

_____

_____

_____

_____

In Mark 2:27, what additional statement does Jesus make before declaring Himself to be the "Lord even of the Sabbath"? What fatal flaw in the legalistic, religious mind-set of the religious leaders and their doctrine did this statement reveal?

_____

_____

_____

_____

_____

Read Matthew 12:9–13. How did the Pharisees next test how far Jesus would go in violating their distorted view of the Sabbath?

_____

_____

_____

_____

How do I describe the basic clash between what legalism values and what God values?

_____

_____

_____

_____

Read Mark 3:6. How did the religious leaders react to what Jesus said and did?

_____

_____

_____

_____

Who were the Herodians? What was so remarkable about the fact that the Pharisees and the Herodians plotted together to try to destroy Jesus?

_____

_____

_____

_____

Which commandment were the Pharisees willing to break just because Jesus offended them about the fourth Commandment about Sabbath?

_____

_____

_____

_____

Jesus understood what the religious leaders clearly did not. The Sabbath is not a rigid, inflexible, complex set of restrictions to be followed. It's really an invitation to be accepted.

How did the elevator button–pushing ban I encountered in Israel come to be?

_____

_____

_____

_____

You can see how creeping legalism can choke all the life and blessing out of God's amazing gift of the Sabbath. I'm not singling out my observant Jewish friends and neighbors here. Some of my fellow Christians have done the same thing. Various Christian denominations have split over issues ranging from baptism to the use of instruments in worship to the presence of a kitchen in the church building.

What examples of this kind of legalism have you observed in the past—not necessarily in the context of the church, but perhaps even within your family or work environment?

_____

_____

_____

_____

We're all capable of giving in to the religious impulse. When we do, we lose the blessing God intends us to experience when we obey from the heart, rather than from mere outward observance of man-made rules.

When we embrace God's principles from the heart, it's not law. It's life!

Are You Ready to Flourish?

Read Psalm 92 in the New King James Version. What is the heading for this Psalm?

_____

_____

_____

_____

What is the purpose of the Sabbath according to verses 1–2?

_____

_____

_____

What is the result of honoring the Lord in this way, according to verse 10?

_____

_____

_____

What is the covering of anointing oil a metaphor for, and why is this such an important concept for a Christian to understand?

_____

_____

_____

Read Exodus 28:3, 31:3, and 35:31. Also read Judges 14:6 and 1 Samuel 16. The Spirit of God resting on men was a big deal throughout the Old Testament. What special gifting did men like Joshua, Samson, and David receive through this anointing?

_____

_____

_____

Keep in mind that this is the Old Covenant era. These people weren't even born again. You and I have the huge advantage of not only having the Spirit of God upon us, but also within us! Nevertheless, Paul wouldn't have exhorted us to continually "be filled with the Spirit" if we didn't need regular "fill-ups" for our tanks.

What will a fresh anointing of the Spirit of God do for us today? How might these benefits be hindered if you've neglected the Sabbath?

_____

_____

_____

_____

What additional benefit of the Sabbath do we see in verses 12 and 14 of Psalm 92?

_____

_____

_____

_____

Read Isaiah 58:13–14 in the New American Standard Version. Describe in your own words how you can be blessed by taking a step of faith to embrace the principle of the Sabbath and making it a priority.

_____

_____

_____

_____

A hundred different things are clamoring for your attention. Your natural impulse—"your own pleasure"—is to attend to those things. If you're a workaholic, "your own pleasure" is to be working. But the wise person steps away.

The Lord encourages us to "call the Sabbath a delight." The Hebrew word here carries the meaning of a luxury. The Sabbath is something we should look forward to, rather than dread. He will provide for all our needs.

What is the reward the psalmist says we will we receive in Psalm 92:14?

_____

_____

_____

_____

Some people think I have a special relationship with the Lord because He often speaks to me. I'm not special. This passage makes it clear. If you want to take more delight in your relationship with the Lord, turn your foot aside from doing your own, busy thing and embrace the Sabbath. "Then," the Word promises us, "you will take delight in the Lord." Or as the New King James translates that verse:

Then you shall delight yourself in the Lord;
And I will cause you to ride on the high hills of the earth,
And feed you with the heritage of Jacob your father.
The mouth of the Lord has spoken.

Read Psalm 37:4. Based on what you have learned so far, how do you delight yourself in the Lord? How do you get to a place where God really is your delight, even if you don't feel that way?

_____

_____

_____

_____

Yes, the Sabbath is your gateway to being that kind of person. As a result, the Lord will "cause you to ride on the high hills of the earth!"

Key Quotes:

"There is something in the fallen human heart that wants to add to the simple instructions God has given us."

"You weren't made for the Sabbath. It was made for you. The Sabbath is a gift."

"Legalism loves the system. God loves people."

"We're all capable of giving in to the religious impulse. When we do, we lose the blessing God intends us to experience when we obey from the heart, rather than from mere outward observance of man-made rules."

"When we embrace God's principles from the heart, it's not law. It's life!"

"Please don't undervalue a fresh anointing of the Spirit of God."

"Turning aside and delighting in the Sabbath brings a great reward."

CHAPTER FIVE

TREAT YOURSELF

We are used to waking up in the morning to begin the day. We know it is important to start our day with a good breakfast. However, Genesis 1:3 makes it clear that the day really begins at sunset.

This is especially true concerning the Sabbath. In observant Jewish households around the world, Friday afternoon is a busy time of preparation for the rapidly approaching twenty-four hours of Sabbath inactivity that will begin with the setting of the sun.

The Sabbath begins with nourishment and then sleep. What is God trying to say about the Sabbath through this pattern?

_____

_____

_____

_____

Many of us wish our children sweet sleep when we put them to bed. That is precisely what King Solomon promised us in Proverbs 3:24–26. According to this passage, how should we feel when we lie down to sleep?

_____

_____

_____

_____

Read Psalm 131:1–2 in the New Living Translation. To what does David compare his soul when he calms and quiets himself?

_____

_____

_____

_____

"Sweet" sleep requires absolute trust in God. Have you ever had a problem with going to sleep? Or awakened in the night with your mind racing so you can't fall back to sleep? I have, and I can tell you why—I wasn't trusting God. Deep in my mind and heart (my soul), I still believed I had to take care of things—to find solutions to my problems.

In general, how quickly and easily do you fall asleep at night? Do you take any aid to help you sleep?

_____

_____

_____

_____

Do you tend to sleep fairly peacefully throughout the night or wake up from time to time? If you wake up, what is usually the reason? What's on your mind at the time you wake? Does it tend to be something that you struggle with on an ongoing basis?

_____

_____

_____

_____

Like during the incident I related in this chapter, you may have trouble sleeping because you're carrying a burden. I was carrying burdens I wasn't meant to carry. Lying awake wrestling with my problems and striving to come up with solutions from my own puny, finite brain revealed a stunning absence of trust in God's faithfulness and a forgetfulness of His immense power.

If you're having difficulty sleeping, it might be because you don't trust God to take care of you. Your mind is too busy working on solutions to all your problems and plotting pathways to all your goals—which brings me back to my point about how the Sabbath begins with the evening. The same posture and attitude that make for a good night's sleep also make for a truly restful Sabbath. First and foremost, it requires trust in your heavenly Father.

What are the thoughts that typically go through your mind as you contemplate taking off a full day each week for the Sabbath?

_____

_____

_____

_____

The Israelites couldn't enter God's rest due to their unbelief. Lack of trust has no place in the heart of a believer. First Peter 5:6–7 tells us, "Therefore humble yourselves under the mighty hand of God, that He may exalt you in due time, casting all your care upon Him, for He cares for you."

Notice the role of humility in this passage. In what ways is pride a major obstacle to entering the rest of the Sabbath?

_____

_____

_____

_____

Read John 15:5. As much as we do not want to feel dependent, the fact is that we *are* dependent on God for *everything*. Anything of lasting value you ever do will be done through your living, breathing connection to the Life of God through His Son, Jesus Christ. That's what makes our refusal to trust God in every area of our lives—including our work lives—so wrongheaded and tragic.

Read Matthew 6:31–34. Trust. Believe. Sleep sweetly. Rest deeply. You can because the God who loves you is faithful, good, and strong.

Three Reasons to Rest

In both 2016 and 2017, the average life expectancy in America dropped, an event that had not occurred in the previous hundred years.[1] We are no longer the longest-living nation in the world. What caused this reversal? A report by the *British Medical Journal* points to two causes: an epidemic of addiction to opioid painkillers and "despair."[2] The author of the study considered it "alarming" that "addiction and the decline in the emotional wellbeing of Americans have been significant enough to drag down the country's average length of life."[3]

Think of your circle of family and friends. Who do you know who works for long hours, day after day, without stopping to rest? Who do you know who might be suffering from a decline in their emotional well-being?

_____

_____

_____

_____

God is serious about rest because He is serious about you. He loves you, and He designed you. The fact is, there are three key reasons we should trust God and embrace a Sabbath rest by setting aside one day each week.

1. A Sabbath gives God the opportunity to provide for us supernaturally.

Exodus 16 illustrates this principle in the way the Lord miraculously provided manna to sustain His people in the wilderness.

How often did the Israelites gather the manna? How much were they supposed to gather? What happened to the manna if they gathered extra and tried to use it the next day?

_____

_____

_____

_____

What did it indicate if a person tried to save manna for the next day?

_____

_____

_____

_____

In verses 23–26 we see God's solution to the problem of gathering manna while not working on the Sabbath. What was that solution?

_____

_____

_____

_____

So this is another lesson for you and me: We shouldn't expect God's supernatural help if we're working seven days a week. If we're going to ignore the Sabbath, we won't find miraculous help, provision, favor, or increase on that seventh day. But if we honor the principle of the Sabbath, we'll find miraculous help on the other six days, and even a double portion of help on the sixth.

As we discovered earlier, this enablement of supernatural provision parallels the principle of the tithe. I'd much rather have 90 percent of my income with God's blessing on it than 100 percent without His blessing. God can accomplish far more in six days that carry God's supernatural blessing than you can in seven without it.

What images of God's creation remind you of His glory and what He can accomplish in six days?

_____

_____

_____

_____

What is true for people is true for businesses as well. While most food chains stay open for seven days a week and sometimes twenty-four hours per day to maximize revenue, Chick-fil-A, the chain founded by born-again believer S. Truett Cathy, has always remained closed on Sundays in order to provide its employees a day to rest and worship if they choose to do so.

In spite of their closing on Sundays, how do Chick-fil-A's restaurant sales compare to their fast-food competitors?

_____

_____

_____

_____

God is pleading with us, "Trust me! Just watch what I can do through you if you'll embrace my principles and my ways."

2. The Sabbath gives us an opportunity to rest and be refreshed.

Exodus 31:16–17 says:

> Therefore the children of Israel shall keep the Sabbath, to observe the Sabbath throughout their generations as a perpetual covenant. It is a sign between Me and the children of Israel forever; for in six days the Lord made the heavens and the earth, and on the seventh day He rested and was refreshed.

What does it mean when God declares the observance of the Sabbath to be a "perpetual covenant"?

_____

_____

_____

_____

Between whom and to whom is the covenant a sign?

_____

_____

_____

_____

Why was the sign of the Sabbath so important to *future* generations of Israelites? What teaching opportunity would it extend to every parent for every child?

_____

_____

_____

_____

In verse 17, God says something else rather startling about the purpose of the Sabbath. He points back and relates it to His six days of creation.

What does verse 17 say God did on the seventh day of creation?

_____

_____

_____

God was obviously not tired after six days of creative activity. We can understand that the word *rest* here means that God simply ceased His creative activity.

If the omnipotent God can't become weary or depleted, how could he possibly ever need to be refreshed?

What does the Hebrew word *naphash* mean?

_____

_____

Naphash appears elsewhere in the Old Testament. It is used with the modern idea where a human can stop to catch their breath.

How did God create light, the world, and all it contains? Likewise, in Genesis 2:7, how did God make Adam to be a living being?

_____

_____

_____

Yes, for the six days of creation, God had been breathing out. Now, on the seventh day, it was time to *naphash*—to breath in.

If God refreshed Himself, why don't you? Ignoring the perpetual principle of the Sabbath robs you of a wonderful opportunity to breathe—to be refreshed.

In observant Jewish households throughout the centuries, a particular ritual has marked the beginning of Shabbat. Shortly before the sun sinks below the horizon, two candles are lit.

What instances from the Torah do the two candles represent?

_____

_____

_____

_____

Fill in the blanks: It's important to _____. But it's even more important to _____ the Sabbath.

God commanded His people to take a day each week to relax and do nothing. It's hard, especially for us modern folks, to imagine spending a full day that way. But this slowness, quietness, and simplicity is something we desperately need, because the lack of these things is killing us.

3. There are consequences when we don't rest.

Remember the man in Numbers 15 who lost his life for gathering sticks on the Sabbath? Read verses 32–36 again.

Read Acts 5:1–11. Does this punishment Ananias and Sapphira received seem excessive to you? Why or why not? What does verse 11 indicate was the purpose of this event for the church to see?

_____

_____

_____

_____

What parallels can you draw between these two events—the way that justice and punishment were meted out and the purpose of these examples?

_____

_____

_____

_____

The observance of the Sabbath was a critical part of God's grand plan to undo the tragic consequences of Adam's rebellion, and the eternal destinies of every person who would one day be able to call upon the name of the Lord and be saved hinged upon the success of the Israelite nation to survive through fifteen more centuries. If the tribes of Israel died out before the fullness of time, there would be no tribe of Judah, and there would be no Jesus.

The deaths of Ananias and Sapphira came about as a direct result of them lying to God about their financial resources. These resources were to be committed, by all who possessed them, to the development—even the survival—of this infant body of believers. This kind of stewardship was absolutely critical to the survival of the early church.

Besides profaning the Sabbath, which three commandments warranted the death penalty under the law of Moses?

_____

_____

_____

_____

If there were extreme consequences for failing to observe the Sabbath under the Old Covenant, should it surprise us that there are negative consequences if we do so today? I'm not talking about divine punishment. I'm talking about experiencing the natural, negative impacts that God was graciously trying to keep His people from experiencing in the first place. God knew we were not designed to run seven days a week and operate on empty physical, emotional, mental, and spiritual tanks.

In a sense, a lifestyle of ignoring the principle of the Sabbath still carries the death penalty! It's slow suicide.

Unwrap the Gift

Yes, the Sabbath is a gift. It's life, not law. This is precisely what Jesus was communicating when He told the Pharisees, "The Sabbath was made for man, and not man for the Sabbath." Observant Jewish people through the millennia have understood this. There is an ancient Jewish saying that I love: "More than Israel has kept Shabbat, Shabbat has kept Israel."[4]

God is imploring you to give yourself the gift of rest one day each week. Trust God and treat yourself. You'll be astonished at how much more you accomplish and how much more you enjoy the journey.

What one or two things will you do this week to help provide some Sabbath rest?

_____

_____

_____

_____

Key Quotes:

"We think our day begins at sunrise. But God says it begins at sunset."

"You are most vulnerable when you're sleeping. In other words, you have to trust God completely when you sleep."

"God has you begin your day of rest with a good night's sleep because in sleeping you're modeling the posture you should have throughout the Sabbath day."

"If you're having difficulty sleeping, it might be because you don't trust God to take care of you."

"Either God's in control or He is not. Either a good God is working all things together for your good or He's not."

"If God refreshed Himself, why don't you?"

"Ignoring the 'perpetual' principle of the Sabbath robs you of a wonderful opportunity to breathe—to be refreshed."

"In a sense, a lifestyle of ignoring the principle of the Sabbath still carries the death penalty! It's slow suicide."

CHAPTER SIX

THE GETAWAY

As we've already seen, when God was creating the laws and covenant ordinances specifically designed to create a successful Israelite society, He put in place very specific rules about giving farm soil a whole year off every seventh year. Leviticus 25:5 says, "What grows of its own accord of your harvest you shall not reap, nor gather the grapes of your untended vine, for it is a year of rest for the land."

The Hebrew term for this Sabbath year for the land was called *shmita*, which means "release." This seventh year is also called the "sabbatical year," or "year of release" (see Deuteronomy 31:10).

Did this *shmita* rest apply only to the land? Who or what else also got a year off?

_____

_____

_____

_____

God cares about animals and flowers. He's *that* good and *that* loving, but He cares infinitely more about us. The fact is, the Sabbath and *shmita* laws are both expressions of that goodness and love. He's not trying to make things harder for His people; He's trying to help us!

Read Leviticus 25:18–19. What two things does the passage say are the result of our obedience?

_____

_____

_____

According to verses 20–22, how much abundance would the land bring forth in the *shmita* year? How long would it last? What was the purpose of that additional blessing?

Of course, all these blessings were predicated on the Israelite tribes' obedience in crossing over into the land of promise.

To *Shmita*, or Not to *Shmita*, That Is the Question

In my story of the Smiths and Joneses, what was the effect on the land of the Smith family because they chose to continue to farm the land each seventh (*shmita*) year?

_____

_____

_____

_____

What was the effect on the land of the Jones family when they let the land lie fallow in the *shmita* year?

_____

_____

_____

_____

What additional benefits to the community took place because of how the Jones family honored the *shmita* year?

_____

_____

_____

_____

This principle of release applied to more than just the land. According to Deuteronomy 25:1–4, what else was to be released every seven years?

_____

_____

_____

_____

In the story above, I suggested we fast-forward fifty years to see how the families were doing.

Interestingly enough, God also had even more than just a seven-year release plan.

Read Leviticus 25:8–17. After seven Sabbath years, what did God proclaim for the fiftieth year? How was that proclaimed to the people?

_____

_____

_____

_____

The English word *jubilee* comes from the Hebrew word *yovel*, meaning trumpet or ram's horn. The sound of the ram's horn announced the beginning of the year of Jubilee on the tenth day of the seventh month. This is known as the Day of Atonement (Yom Kippur).

Read Acts 2:1. On what day did the Holy Spirit come and breathe fresh life into the newly formed church of believers?

_____

_____

What does *Pentecost* mean? What relationship or parallels can you see between the Year of Jubilee, beginning on the Day of Atonement of the fiftieth year, and the meaning or symbolism of what took place at Pentecost?

_____

_____

_____

_____

The Power of a Sabbatical

God gave Israel both the Sabbath *and* the *shmita*. There is a place for both in our lives today. The English word *sabbatical* is rooted in the Hebrew word *shabbat*, and somewhere along the way was transliterated into the Latin word *sabbaticus* and the Greek word *sabbatikos*—all of which generally refer to taking an extended rest. Our current concept of a sabbatical is rooted in the biblical practice of *shmita*.

Few people can afford to take a full year away from their jobs. However, for Stefan Sagmeister, a renowned artist and designer in New York, it seemed like what he needed to do. In 2001, he shut down his company and wandered around Southeast Asia for an entire year.

What were Sagmeister's concerns or fears about his decision to take the year off based upon his comments in 2009?

_____

_____

_____

What did Sagmeister concentrate on during his yearlong wandering?

_____

_____

_____

What happened to his business when he returned? What awards did he win?

_____

_____

_____

What did Sagmeister list as the four positive effects of his sabbatical?

_____

_____

To my knowledge, Sagmeister is neither Jewish nor Christian. Yet by daring to take a yearlong sabbatical, he intuitively activated an ancient wisdom principle in God's Word—the principle of the *shmita*. It is a practice he continues to this day.

Again, very few of us can afford to take an entire year off. However, you and I can incorporate sabbaticals into our twenty-first-century lives.

More than a Vacation

Remember that we're applying a principle here, not a law. The *shmita* principle is that periodic extended breaks from being "productive" can have a powerful restorative effect on body, soul, and spirit.

How long did it take for a sabbatical to make me right when God led me to first apply this principle?

What is the nature and purpose of the sabbatical policy we implemented for our pastoral staff, and more recently for some of our nonpastoral staff, at Gateway Church?

I know not everyone can manage an unbroken six-week stretch away from work. However, even an extra week or two of extended, unplugged rest every few years can work wonders.

Please understand, I'm not talking about simply taking a vacation. Frankly, the way many people do vacations, they end up more exhausted than if they'd kept working. How many times have you heard someone say, "I need a vacation to recover from my vacation!"?

What type of vacation do you typically take? Road trips or action-packed trips to exotic destinations? Extended rests at the beach or a mountain cabin?

_____

_____

_____

_____

Do you have an example of when you came back from a vacation feeling particularly refreshed and invigorated? How about one where you came back feeling worn out and tired from travel?

_____

_____

_____

_____

A sabbatical is both more and less than a vacation. Yet a vacation—even a tiring one—is at least a change of scenery. Many of us aren't even taking vacations anymore. The trend in this country is to leave paid vacation unused, and people are doing this to a greater degree than in the past.

Based upon the Project Time Off study,[1] how much vacation time does the average employee take each year? What has been the trend in recent years?

_____

_____

_____

_____

Fewer vacation days is not even a win for the companies who employ them. Increasingly, businesses are realizing that having a burned-out, stressed-out, weary, mentally fuzzy, emotionally fragile workforce isn't exactly a great thing for productivity and efficiency.

According to the 2018 U.S. Travel Association study,[2] what is the effect upon employees' relationships, health, and well-being when they use most or all of their vacation days?

_____

_____

_____

_____

When you do take a vacation, do you tend to still monitor email and developments at work when you are gone? Why? Do you think it is helpful?

_____

_____

_____

_____

The Modified Sabbatical

There is not just one correct way to do a sabbatical.

Back in the 1980s, Bill Gates discovered the power of going away and being alone for a week in a remote place once a year. Gates annually retreated to a tiny cabin on a largely uninhabited island off the coast of Washington State accessible only by seaplane. These weeks became vital times to step away from the constant cyclone of meetings, decisions, and day-to-day details and look at the bigger picture. These came to be called "think weeks," and they became a regular part of Microsoft's culture.

What were some of the specific ideas or results that came out of Bill Gates's think weeks?

_____

_____

_____

_____

Bill Gates and others have stumbled onto a spiritual principle that works. But sabbaticals are so much more powerful when you add the element of the Spirit of God to the equation. That's exactly what one of the most successful Christian businessmen I've ever known started doing years ago. In fact, he'll tell you his regular sabbaticals are a major reason he was so wildly successful in business.

In my previous books *The Blessed Life* and *Beyond Blessed*, I shared stewardship stories about my good friend Steve Dulin, who is also one of the founding elders at Gateway Church.

What I've never shared is that one of his most powerful secrets to making wise business decisions is the sabbatical. Steve is a passionate and persuasive advocate of taking regular, weeklong stretches alone, away from the demands and distractions of daily work life.

In what ways is Steve's sabbatical time like Bill Gates's think weeks? How is it different, and what is the reason behind that difference?

_____

_____

_____

_____

How did Steve apply the principle of the sabbatical once he discovered their power? Where did he go? What did he do and *not* do?

_____

_____

_____

_____

What kinds of ideas and decisions came out of Steve's sabbatical seasons with God?

_____

_____

_____

_____

In your own words, why do you think these times contributed to Steve's success?

_____

_____

_____

_____

Look at and consider Steve's list of eighteen keys to a successful Sabbath. What is your immediate impression of the list?

_____

_____

_____

_____

Which of these things, if any, do you regularly practice? Why? Have they helped you?

_____

_____

_____

How might you plan to implement some or all of these principles into your life?

_____

_____

_____

A Sabbatical for Your Most Important Relationship

Another key member of Gateway's leadership team has long championed a special variation of the classic sabbatical. One of our founding elders, the founder of the global marriage enrichment ministry MarriageToday, Jimmy Evans, recommends that couples take a sabbatical together periodically to do much the same kind of thing.

Jimmy knows and teaches that married couples have much stronger relationships and build healthier, more successful families when they have a shared vision and hear from God together. And the best way to do that is to periodically take what he calls a "vision retreat"—a sabbatical for couples.

What are the elements Jimmy suggests should be incorporated into a vision retreat?

_____

_____

_____

What are the likely outcomes of a couple's sabbatical?

_____

_____

_____

If you are married, have you ever been on a marriage retreat of any kind? What were the results? Which of the elements in the list did you incorporate in the retreat?

_____

_____

_____

If you are not married, do you know of couples who have been on a marriage retreat? What were the results to your knowledge?

_____

_____

_____

A sabbatical, whether as a couple or alone, is a powerful thing—especially when you add God to the mix.

Unleashing Supernatural Creativity

Jesus only had a three-year ministry. As the gospels reveal, it was surely one of the busiest, most intense three years any human has ever experienced. He ping-ponged back and forth across the land of Israel, preaching, teaching, and healing in every village and synagogue in the land. Not only was Jesus constantly in demand and surrounded by crowds, but the invisible spiritual warfare surrounding Him must have been beyond our ability to imagine. It's no exaggeration to say that no human being in history ever had a more demanding and draining three-year run than did Jesus of Nazareth.

How did Jesus launch his ministry immediately after His baptism? How long was His sabbatical time in the desert, and what did it involve?

_____

_____

_____

_____

Throughout Jesus' ministry, what was His attitude toward taking time away from His grueling schedule? What does that imply as to how we should view this kind of rest today?

_____

_____

_____

_____

Especially if you're older, have you noticed that forgetfulness and inability to focus hamper your creativity and critical thinking? Give an example.

_____

_____

_____

_____

Have you had the kind of experience where you have a hard time remembering something, no matter how hard you try, and then all of a sudden, a few minutes later or after a night's sleep, the answer or idea pops into your head? Give an example.

_____

_____

_____

_____

If just a tiny sliver of quiet, disengagement, or rest can give you little breakthroughs like that, imagine what an extended period with those things could do for your mind.

Does the idea of taking an extended sabbatical sound boring? Why?

_____

_____

_____

Why are we often bored? Uncomfortable with silence?

_____

_____

_____

What do the research mentioned and examples cited suggest about the link between stillness and inactivity (boredom) and creative breakthroughs?

_____

_____

_____

Read Psalm 23:1–3 in the Passion Translation. Ponder this song of praise for a moment. Describe what the Holy Spirit reveals in this passage about what blessings extended time alone with God can provide.

_____

_____

_____

_____

Key Quotes:

"The fact is, the Sabbath and *shmita* laws are both expressions of that goodness and love. He's not trying to make things harder for His people; He's trying to help us!"

"The *shmita* principle is that periodic extended breaks from being 'productive' can have a powerful restorative effect on body, soul, and spirit."

"How out of balance are we as a culture when many of us won't stay home even when they'll pay us to do it?"

"A sabbatical is an extended period of quiet, stillness, rest, reflection, prayer, and fellowship with God and His Word."

"Couples have much stronger relationships and build healthier, more successful families when they have a shared vision and hear from God together."

"That's what makes a sabbatical so powerful and so very important. Among its many blessings and benefits, it restores and replenishes your creativity."

"Nothing is more refreshing than communion with God."

CHAPTER SEVEN

TOP PRIORITY

We all have our priorities. We tend to spend our time, just as we do our money, in accordance with what we value most. Back when people wrote checks, I used to say, "Show me your checkbook register, and I'll show you what you truly value." The same is true of your calendar. The problem is, we don't always value the right things.

You'll recall Stephen Covey's illustration about the "big rocks." We learned that if you don't put the big rocks in first, you'll never fit them in at all. The takeaway for us here is that if you want to make a Sabbath rest a regular part of your life, you're going to have to make it a priority. The time for rest won't just appear magically. There must be a plan to prioritize rest along with all the other rocks that you want to go in your jar.

Consider your personal life and schedule. List some of the activities and roles you juggle. What kinds of issues and stresses occur from trying to juggle and fulfill those activities and roles?

_____

_____

_____

_____

What do you consider the top two or three roles or activities on the list you just made? What portion of your time do you end up spending on those?

_____

_____

In financial terms, as I noted when I dealt with stewardship in my book *Beyond Blessed*, the budget is the vital tool for becoming a better steward of money. The counterpart to the budget when it comes to the management of our time is the schedule.

How did Stephen Covey express the appropriate thought process to deal with priorities on your schedule?

_____

_____

_____

Goals are not real unless they move from your heart and mind to your calendar. How useful are to-do lists for scheduling and managing priorities? Why?

_____

_____

_____

Your calendar is your budget for stewarding your time. Most of us tend to think of our calendars as things where only appointments and meetings are noted. Most of these revolve around our 8:00 a.m. to 6:00 p.m. workdays, but the reality is that the world will rush in to fill all the blank spaces.

I once heard a pastor friend of mine ask a large gathering of fellow pastors, "How would you spend your time if God were in charge of your calendar?"

How did this pastor describe the proper method of evaluating whether we are using our calendars effectively?

_____

_____

_____

Your calendar or schedule should be a detailed and accurate reflection of *who you want to become*, rather than just filled with *stuff you want to get done*. There's something powerful and activating about having a thing on your schedule. It moves it from the realm of the hypothetical to the realm of the real. Things on your calendar become real.

What was the advice from my successful writer friend to get started writing? What simple step did John Grisham take to get committed to focus on writing?

_____

_____

_____

_____

Putting something on your calendar moves it from being a *wish* to being an *appointment*. Time is allocated.

This is no less true when it comes to rest. If you want to be a rested person—a person who recognizes and honors the wisdom of the principle of the Sabbath—then you'll need to have a standing appointment with *rest*. We need to understand this like the pastor friend with whom I tried to schedule a Thursday lunch years ago.

Making Tough Choices

The moment you decide to make a Sabbath rest a priority and plant that flag on your schedule, I can promise you'll immediately get a steady stream of opportunities to compromise that decision. Every one of those requests will be sincere, legitimate, and worthwhile. The fact is, in any given hour of any given day, there are thousands of "good" things you could be doing. Yet you can only do one thing at a time. You cannot do all the things. We have to *choose*. And you *will* choose.

List the things I mention that can drive your choice of what to do. Add some others if you can think of them.

_____

_____

_____

_____

What is the term Stephen Covey uses to describe the critical factor that must drive how we make choices? How does Covey describe the control that we have over our lives and how our decisions affect our lives?

_____

_____

_____

_____

Once you've made the decision to incorporate God's wisdom concerning rest into your weekly life, you're going to have to learn to defend and protect that decision. I now deliberately and intentionally schedule time to cultivate the nonnegotiable priorities of my life: God, my family, my work, and my health. I budget specific blocks of time for these things.

What is the benefit of consistently scheduling what is important rather than leaving things to chance or good intentions?

_____

_____

_____

_____

Money and time are both important resources that require our stewardship to be an effective ambassador of God's kingdom.

How was Mr. Budget characterized in the early years of the Morris family household? How did we use him to make decisions?

_____

_____

_____

_____

Mr. Budget has an ally in the daily battle to stay true to your goals and values: "Mr. Schedule." That is basically what my friend was doing all those years ago when I was trying to talk him into having lunch with me on his Sabbath. He was saying, "Robert, I'd love to get some time with you, but next Thursday is out. I asked 'Mr. Schedule,' and he said I'm booked all that day. Booked doing 'nothing'!"

Putting First Things First

There are only twenty-four hours in a day, and as we noted earlier, we can't make time or save time. Therefore, saying yes to the things that are most important will almost certainly require saying no to several, perhaps many, worthwhile things.

What is the brutally honest method of critique required when trying to steward finances using a budget or trying to steward time using a schedule?

_____

_____

_____

_____

One of the most powerful ways to increase your available reserves of both time and money is to *simplify*.

Why do you think it is important to simplify our lives? Why are they so complicated in the first place?

_____

_____

_____

_____

Describe what we lose in life through complexity and what we gain through simplicity.

_____

_____

_____

_____

You'll need to schedule rest and protect your schedule if you're going to capture the life-giving power of honoring the Sabbath principle. Scheduling rest helps me in multiple ways. There are the natural, physical benefits of rest we've explored in some depth in the previous chapters. Yet there is much more going on here. Being deliberate about honoring a Sabbath day of rest is an expression of my trust and faith in God.

How is being deliberate about the Sabbath day of rest an expression of trust and faith in God? How difficult is it for you to come to grips with this notion?

_____

_____

_____

_____

Take some time to think about your need for dependency on God. Read Pastor Brady Boyd's comments and then express, in your own words, your need to rest in that dependency.

_____

_____

_____

_____

Read John 15:5. What does this verse remind us about the source of our ability to accomplish anything in life—to bear fruit for Him?

_____

_____

_____

_____

Do you enjoy the feeling of accomplishment from hard work? How easy is it for you to make the internal shift back into "work mode"?

_____

_____

_____

_____

Explain and respond to this statement: God doesn't need my work; He wants *me*.

_____

_____

_____

_____

God isn't seated in heaven handing out "gold stars." He already stamped you and me with His approval in Jesus Christ through His Holy Spirit. A Sabbath gives you and me an opportunity to recalibrate our relationship with God and rediscover who we are in Him.

By observing the Sabbath, I declare, "You are God and I am not." God designed us to rest, enjoy Him, and receive from His unending supply of grace. The Sabbath is good for us. But observing it runs completely counter to the fallen human nature and to the prideful spirit of this age.

Common Questions

What day of the week can your Sabbath be on? What is the important principle of power behind the decision to enjoy Sabbath?

_____

_____

_____

_____

What should you do on your Sabbath? My simple answer is "Enjoy! Enjoy your life. Enjoy your heavenly Father. Enjoy your family."

Does the Sabbath have to involve just religious activities, such as Bible study and prayer? How would that attitude today compare with the attitude of the Pharisees toward the Sabbath? What were they focused on? What should we be focused on?

_____

_____

_____

_____

This is why I told the man who asked me about golf that, as long as he could afford it and not neglect his family, he could enjoy golf on his Sabbath. Whatever nourishes your soul and refreshes and invigorates your body...do it. Just do it _with_ God. Make Him a part of your day, all day long.

What is the short answer to the question, "What should I not do on the Sabbath?"

_____

_____

Describe in more detail how the boundaries between work-time and home-time have been erased. What is the most important thing to do to help unplug ourselves from work?

_____

_____

_____

What should be our attitude toward social media on our Sabbath day? What are some of the reasons social media is so destructive to rest?

_____

_____

_____

Do you feel that you hear God? How does He speak to you? How can we use the Sabbath to learn to hear God more clearly and more often?

_____

_____

_____

What about an emergency? Read Luke 14:5 and 13:15 and Matthew 12:12. What should you consider doing if emergencies continue to interrupt your Sabbath on a regular basis?

_____

_____

_____

Read Psalm 95. Describe the role of worship in entering God's supernatural rest. What are some examples of attributes of God we should reflect on? What are some of His fundamental promises He wants us to experience and enjoy?

_____

_____

_____

_____

Refilling Your Tanks

A proper Sabbath will help restore you spiritually, physically, emotionally, and mentally.

How can we refill our spiritual tank?

Prayer and reading Scripture are obvious starting points. Declaring the truth about God and His goodness out loud helps lift our inner spirit. Angels snap to attention and demons tremble when they hear us.

Ask the Holy Spirit to direct you to passages of Scripture that apply specifically to areas of weakness or struggle in your life. It may help to study those passages in different translations.

What are specific areas of weakness or struggle for which you can seek help from God at this time in your life?

_____

_____

_____

_____

Prayer can sometimes be difficult but is enormously powerful. Jesus reopened that pathway of direct communication with God that Adam and Eve forfeited by their rebellion.

Do you find praying difficult? If so, explain how you feel and why.

_____

_____

_____

_____

What kinds of things can you share directly with God? Are there any limitations? Is there any reason God would not respond to you in an unconditionally loving way?

_____

_____

_____

_____

Do you ever engage in fasting? What is your opinion about fasting? What are the potential benefits of fasting? What would you fast from?

_____

_____

_____

_____

What would be the top area of focus for you to fill your spiritual tank?

_____

_____

_____

_____

How can we refill our physical tank?

Our physical tank is often the one in which we notice the deficit first.

What refills your physical tank will depend on the kind of work and activities you pursue. It can vary from week to week.

What are some examples of ways to refill your physical tank? What part does exercise play?

_____

_____

_____

_____

Focus on Christ and allow Him to show you how to recharge your body. What would be the top area of focus for you to refill your physical tank?

_____

_____

_____

_____

How can we refill our emotional tank?

Like with your physical tank, what refills your emotional tank will vary greatly depending on your personality and interests.

What kinds of things can build us up and fill our emotional tank?

_____

_____

_____

_____

What things should we look out for that easily drain our emotional tank?

_____

_____

_____

_____

Read Philippians 4:8. What kinds of things in general should we focus on during our Sabbath?

_____

_____

_____

_____

What would be the top area of focus for you to refill your emotional tank?

How can we refill our mental tank?

There is something wonderful about creating space to think—not strategically mull over problems or mentally rehearse upcoming conversations. Just...think.

Review some of the options for mental stimulation that were listed near the end of Chapter 3.

What would be the top area of focus for you to refill your mental tank?

Ask the Lord to inspire your imagination and let your mind wander. It's refreshing!

If you will make the Sabbath a priority and protect it—in the words of Isaiah, if you will make it your delight—God will meet you in that day in a powerful and refreshing way.

He will faithfully provide for you spiritually, physically, emotionally, and mentally if only you'll trust Him enough to simply rest.

Key Quotes:

"If you want to make a Sabbath rest a regular part of your life, you're going to have to make it a priority."

"Your calendar is your budget for stewarding your time."

"If it isn't scheduled, it isn't a real goal. It's nothing more than a good intention."

"With time, just as with money, planning is vital. If you don't create a plan, our fallen, broken world will create one for you."

"When we simplify our lives, we gain wealth."

"Without our connection to Jesus, we're not capable of doing anything of eternal value."

"One of the powerful and important aspects of a full day of unplugged, disconnected, undistracted Sabbath rest is that you can actually *hear* God."

CHAPTER EIGHT

IT'S NOT ALL ABOUT YOU

How much of yourself—or of someone close to you—do you see in the story of Zac and Rebecca?

_____

_____

_____

_____

Outward-Spreading Ripples

Zac and Rebecca—a composite of many people I've known over the years rolled into one fictionalized couple—were suffering from a severe case of Sabbath deficiency syndrome. In other words, they were chronically tired. They had each been running for too long on four near-empty tanks. They were living without margin.

What this story illustrates is that Zac and Rebecca were not the only ones impacted by their failure to understand the power and importance of Sabbath rest.

How was Zac and Rebecca's perpetual exhaustion affecting how they related to each other?

_____

_____

To their children?

What were some of the potential long-term effects of their behaviors on their marriage and family?

What happened to the relationships that Zac and Rebecca had with their coworkers? How did they appear different to those around them?

What happened to their job performance?

Have you or someone close to you ever experienced these types of changes in relationships based upon constant weariness and fatigue? Explain.

Although they couldn't have imagined it, chronic stress and weariness were compromising their health and actually shortening their life spans. God had planned for both to live long, productive lives in His service, impacting tens of thousands of people for the kingdom along the way. God's highest and best for them was to fulfill the promise of Psalm 91:16: "With long life I will satisfy him and show him my salvation."

Summarize the effect that Zac and Rebecca's weariness was having on their future and their legacy.

_____

_____

_____

_____

What this illustration brings home is that while Sabbath rest is vitally important for you and your life, it's just as important to those around you.

The more you discover about the kingdom of God, the more you learn it's never all about you. If you're not resting regularly and deeply, you're not being the best person you can be. This, in turn, affects all areas of your life, everyone in your sphere of influence, and even eternity itself. It's that big a deal.

A Message to the World

God told the Israelites that the Sabbath was a sign and a message.
Of what was the Sabbath a sign?

_____

_____

_____

_____

Of what was the Sabbath a message?

_____

_____

_____

_____

How is this message about the Sabbath the same for you and me today?

Matthew 5:14–16 says, "You are the light of the world. A city that is set on a hill cannot be hidden. Nor do they light a lamp and put it under a basket, but on a lampstand, and it gives light to all who are in the house. Let your light so shine before men, that they may see your good works and glorify your Father in heaven."

How does this passage apply to us today? How does our good, happy, peaceful life speak to others?

_____

_____

_____

_____

Yes, honoring the Sabbath speaks to the world. And the supernatural power and blessings that come from honoring the Sabbath speak to the world as well. One of the greatest testaments to that truth I've ever heard comes by way of a Christian-owned company during World War II.

Convictions Tested

"How many boats can you make in nineteen days?"

These were the words on the urgent telegram that landed on February 9, 1945, on the desk of Ralph Meloon, the head of Correct Craft, a small but growing ski boat manufacturing factory in Pine Castle, Florida. The sender of the telegram was the US Army combat engineers, asking on behalf of General Dwight D. Eisenhower, supreme allied commander of the Allied Expeditionary Forces battling Nazi Germany on the other side of the Atlantic.

What were the special requirements of these boats, and why were they needed so urgently?

_____

_____

_____

_____

Correct Craft ordinarily turned out about forty-eight boats per month (roughly twelve boats per week, or two per day).

What action did Ralph Meloon take with his family before he committed his company to produce three hundred of the specialized boats in less than three weeks?

_____

_____

_____

_____

Besides the decision to produce the boats in the first place, what major considerations did Meloon need to make about the weekly production schedule?

_____

_____

_____

_____

What did the government advisors tell him would be required of the production schedule of Correct Craft to meet the deadline?

_____

_____

_____

_____

How much consideration did Meloon and the company give to the question of whether or not to work on Sunday? How did they express their decision not to work on Sunday to the advisors? What would they have done if the government had insisted on Sunday work?

_____

_____

_____

_____

How many boats did they produce in the first three workdays?

_____

_____

_____

_____

What did Mr. Meloon and his family do after the end of the third day of production? What was the result of that action?

_____

_____

_____

_____

Remember the two other boat companies that had been contracted to fulfill the rest of General Eisenhower's request? They were falling behind, even though they were running three shifts, seven days per week. So, the government asked Mr. Meloon if his company could manage an additional one hundred boats by the deadline, upping their total to *four hundred*. He said yes, and they made it happen. In fact, the entire order was delivered ahead of time.

On the night of March 23, 1945, under cover of heavy artillery bombardment and close air support by the Royal Air Force, the four hundred storm boats crafted only weeks earlier by Ralph Meloon's Sabbath-honoring workforce carried thousands of American soldiers into German territory.

What was the problem with the boats made by the other manufacturers that rendered them unfit for the mission?

_____

_____

_____

_____

What recognition did Correct Craft receive for their efforts? What term did the press use to describe the company's manufacturing feat?

_____

_____

_____

_____

How has Correct Craft prospered since that time?

_____

_____

_____

How old was the founder, Ralph C. Meloon, Sr., when he passed away?

_____

_____

_____

Mr. Meloon knew what you and I need to understand. There is nothing quite like doing things God's way. In the busiest and most stressful times, God will bless your work when you go about it His way. Just as importantly, it will testify to a watching world that God is real, and He is faithful.

The World Is Watching (and Tasting)

Matthew 5–7 presents, at length, one of Jesus' first sermons. We know it as the Sermon on the Mount. At the time the Lord delivered this message, He had only recently walked out of the desert after spending forty days there fasting and being tested. Yes, tested. Jesus, on your behalf and mine, passed the very same test that our ancestor, Adam, failed.

Describe the different outcomes of Adam's encounter with Satan compared to Jesus' encounter with him.

_____

_____

_____

What were the differences in the circumstances (conditions and location) between Adam's and Jesus' encounter with Satan?

_____

_____

Adam lacked nothing. Jesus lacked everything. Even so, Jesus remained faithful to God and to His mission. It's no accident that in two different New Testament books, the apostle Paul explains that Jesus is "the Last Adam"—sent by God to undo the damage the first Adam had done. (See Romans 5:12–21; 1 Corinthians 15:20–28, 47–49.)

Matthew 5:13–16 provides vivid imagery of how a believer's life should influence those around him:

> You are the salt of the earth; but if the salt loses its flavor, how shall it be seasoned? It is then good for nothing but to be thrown out and trampled underfoot by men.
>
> You are the light of the world. A city that is set on a hill cannot be hidden. Nor do they light a lamp and put it under a basket, but on a lampstand, and it gives light to all *who are* in the house. Let your light so shine before men, that they may see your good works and glorify your Father in heaven.

First, Jesus says that we believers are salt.

According to Leviticus 2:13 and Numbers 18:19, with what substance were grain offerings and heave offerings seasoned?

_____

_____

_____

Keep in mind that everything God had the Israelites do in the Old Testament carried special meaning and symbolic significance. There are no insignificant details in the instructions God gave to Israel. Everything either pointed to Jesus or to what Jesus would establish in the New Covenant. So when we hear God say the "salt of the covenant" and the "covenant of salt," we should take notice.

What's He pointing to here? Well, for one thing, salt preserves. It has been used to preserve food for millennia.

What does it mean, in spiritual terms, for salt to preserve? How long does it preserve and how is the covenant involved?

_____

_____

_____

_____

Read Psalm 97:10 and Proverbs 16:17. How is the *perseverance* of the saints related to the *preservation* of the saints?

_____

_____

_____

_____

We have three scriptural witnesses all testifying to the fact that God preserves us if we belong to Him. That tells me my connection to God isn't dependent upon *my* sticking power. It's dependent on God's covenantal faithfulness.

According to Deuteronomy 7:9 and Psalm 105:8, for how long will God remember and keep His covenant?

_____

_____

God's preserving power isn't just for this present life. It's eternal. God preserves your soul forever. You're going to live forever because of the covenant you have with God through Jesus Christ.

It may sound dramatic, but it's no exaggeration to say that God's people are preserving the world. Adam unleashed decay and death into the world, but our presence is keeping that decay at bay.

In what ways, when you look at various cultures throughout the world, do we see how God's people are "preserving the world"?

_____

_____

_____

What will be the effect of our culture's rejection of Christian faith principles?

Jesus also said that we are light. Of course, on more than one other occasion, Jesus said He, Himself, was the light of the world. How can we reconcile that? Is He the light of the world, or are we?

It makes perfect sense when you understand that, on this side of the cross, we are *in* Jesus and Jesus is *in* us. **We are His body and can do "more" than He did.** That is what He prayed for in John 17:20–21.

That is why we are the light of the world. The true light of the world is in us, and we are, at the same time, in Him. The fact is, you and I are the only light this world has.

Of what important truth does John 1:5 remind us?

We are salt and we are light. We preserve and we illuminate. We prevent corruption and dispel darkness. We make life taste better, and we show the way.

What warning did Jesus give about when salt loses its saltiness?

What warning did Jesus give about what happens when you cover up a lamp with a basket?

_____

_____

_____

_____

In both cases, Jesus is saying that, as salt and light, your role is to preserve and illuminate. And if you're not doing that, you're failing at a fundamental reason God has you in this world.

Explain how failing to observe the principle of the Sabbath leads to Christians losing their preserving impact on the world. What are the results?

_____

_____

_____

_____

Step Up by Stepping Away

How does a refusal to rest and recharge rob you and those around you of the good life God wants you to experience?

_____

_____

_____

_____

For some of those who cross your path, what might hinge on encountering the rested version of you?

_____

_____

_____

_____

Key Quotes:

"While Sabbath rest is vitally important for you and your life, it's just as important to those around you."

"Honoring the Sabbath speaks to the world. And the supernatural power and blessings that come from honoring the Sabbath, speak to the world as well."

"In the busiest and most stressful times, God will bless your work when you go about it His way."

"God's preserving power isn't just for this present life. It's eternal. God preserves your soul forever. You're going to live forever because of the covenant you have with God through Jesus Christ."

"We are salt and we are light. We preserve and we illuminate. We prevent corruption and dispel darkness. We make life taste better, and we show the way."

"The fact is, for some who cross your path, their eternal destinies actually hinge on encountering the rested version of you."

CHAPTER NINE

REST AND HUMILITY

As we've seen, there are many reasons Christians don't fully incorporate the blessing of Sabbath rest into their lives. In fact, it often seems like the whole world is conspiring to keep us busy, stressed, distracted, and on the move. The culture doesn't want you to rest. The enemy of your soul certainly doesn't want you to rest. And often, *we* don't really want to rest.

Fear and greed are important forces that hinder our ability to pursue Sabbath. But what is the primary factor standing between God's people and the blessings of Sabbath rest?

_____

_____

_____

_____

Embracing the rest of the Sabbath requires both a recognition that we are dependent upon God *and* a willingness to be dependent on Him. Pride will allow neither of these. Simply put, there is something deeply embedded in the fallen man that wants to say, "Look at me! I did this myself!"

In other words, we want *glory*. We want to be *glorified* in the eyes of others. This was Lucifer's catastrophic conceit. He wasn't satisfied with reflecting God's glory. He wanted the glory for himself.

According to Matthew 5:16, what is the purpose of letting our light shine so that people see our good works?

_____

_____

_____

This is why God made such a big deal of the Sabbath for His Old Covenant people.

What was the Sabbath a sign of, relative to His people?

_____

_____

_____

How was the Sabbath also a sign to foreigners?

_____

_____

_____

Read Isaiah 42:8. How much of the glory does God want to have?

_____

_____

_____

_____

Abram's Nap

How old was Abram when God first approached him?

_____

What was God's promise to Abram?

_____

_____

_____

_____

_____

What was required of Abram to receive God's promise?

_____

_____

_____

A Rest Remains

Why did God put Abram to sleep during the covenant ceremony? Why did such a solemn ceremony require a proxy for Abram's side of the covenant?

_____

_____

_____

What was the Abrahamic Covenant a forerunner of?

_____

_____

_____

There is no way we sinful, fallen humans could enter into a covenant of promise with a pure and holy God. So, God sent us a proxy, His Son, Jesus, to walk "between the pieces" for us. Yes, back during Abram's nap, that was the son of God standing in for him, walking side by side with God through those animal halves.

What is the Hebrew term used to define both the deep sleep God put Adam into when He made Eve and the sleep that fell on Abram during the ceremony?

_____

_____

When God is trying to do something that only He can do, our part is always to rest and trust. Yes, we must obey when God gives us an instruction. Abram had to obey God's directive to get the animals necessary for the covenant ceremony. But when it comes to bringing about the results of God's covenant promises, God wants us in a posture of rest.

Why does God want us in a posture of rest in these situations?

Look again at Hebrews 4:9, 11 as we examine this truth further: "There remains therefore a rest for the people of God. . . . Let us therefore be diligent to enter that rest."

Hebrews makes the case to Jewish people that the New Covenant in Jesus is superior in every way to the Old Covenant—with better promises and a better High Priest. In Chapter 3, verses 7–11, the writer begins to warn his Jewish readers that they are facing a decision very similar to the one faced by their ancestors who were camped on the edge of the promised land.

These New Testament hearers faced the same decision the Israelites did. They can believe the proclamation of the Word of God about Jesus, accept Him, and enter into the restful promised land of new birth in the kingdom of God. Or through unbelief, they can be like that generation about which God declared, "They will never enter my place of rest" (3:11). Chapter 3 closes with these words: "So we see that because of their unbelief they were not able to enter His rest" (NLT).

Again, embracing the principle of the Sabbath is a step of faith.

Yet there is a another, very important dimension to the Sabbath.

Shabbat-ing from Dead Works

In Hebrews 4:10 we read that those who entered His rest *"ceased from his works* as God did from His." The Hebrew word here, of course, is *Shabbat*, the root of our word Sabbath.

What does the word *Shabbat* mean?

_____

_____

_____

_____

The writer closes this chapter of Hebrews with this precious and comforting promise:

> Seeing then that we have a great High Priest who has passed through the heavens, Jesus the Son of God, let us hold fast our confession. For we do not have a High Priest who cannot sympathize with our weaknesses, but was in all points tempted as we are, yet without sin. Let us therefore come boldly to the throne of grace, that we may obtain mercy and find grace to help in time of need.

What kind of throne do we approach as believers? What does that mean to you?

_____

_____

_____

_____

The writer sums up this passage about finding rest in the promised land of the New Covenant by saying that this truth is really a basic, foundational truth of the gospel.

Read Hebrews 6:1–2. What does "not laying again the foundation of repentance from dead works" mean? How does the New Covenant that was entered into resemble the one entered into with Abram?

_____

_____

_____

If we try to earn our way into a relationship with God, we will fail. You have to cease (*Shabbat*) your religious labors. Simply believe, and trust in Jesus to hold up your side.

What are the five key points and Scriptures concerning the Sabbath rest and our efforts to qualify for God's acceptance?

_____

_____

_____

_____

Respond to this statement: Entering into the blessings of the New Covenant means, in a sense, going to sleep and letting Jesus walk for you. It also means that you grow fruitful as a believer the same way you became one in the first place—that is, by resting in Jesus' performance of the covenant's requirements. You humbly and gratefully enter it in a position of rest, and you remain in a position of rest.

_____

_____

_____

_____

What is the only part we play in entering into the Sabbath rest? Why does pride hate this? Why won't pride let us accept the free gift Paul writes about in Ephesians 2:8–10?

_____

_____

_____

_____

If we are not saved by our striving and efforts, where do these good works come in?

Good Works Flow *from* Your Connection

Fully embracing the principle of Sabbath goes beyond having faith to do so and being rewarded by God with supernatural increase and provision.

Jesus said to let the world see our good works, and James said that faith without works is dead. We must simply realize that our works don't *earn* us our connection to God; good works are a natural outgrowth of being connected to God.

Good works require resources and effort. God provides both. Sabbath rest replenishes resources.

Read John 15:1, 4–5, 8.

Describe the relationship of bearing fruit to the principle of rest (abiding)? What do we bring to God when we bear fruit?

There remains a Sabbath rest for the people of God. Humble yourself, and in childlike trust, receive that rest. Abide in that rest. Thrive in that rest. Bear much fruit in that rest.

Key Quotes:

"The culture doesn't want you to rest. The enemy of your soul certainly doesn't want you to rest. And often, *we* don't really want to rest."

"The sin of pride is often the primary thing standing between God's people and the blessings of Sabbath rest."

"When God says 'rest,' He means rest."

"Abram discovered that his part in this whole thing was to believe and to *rest*. So important was the resting part that God put him to sleep!"

"Entering into the blessings of the New Covenant means, in a sense, going to sleep and letting Jesus walk your side of the covenant for you."

"We don't do good works *for* our relationship to God; we do them *from* our relationship to Him."

CHAPTER TEN

THE TIME IS NOW

The remarkable success story of W. Clement Stone was built on a number of positive traits and habits, including the power of having a positive mental attitude. But perhaps the most powerful and effective thing Stone gave his salespeople was a simple key to overcoming procrastination.

Fear of rejection, stress, and discouragement will fuel procrastination. They make it easy to rationalize delay. Stone knew he needed a way to help his salespeople break through in the critical moment of indecision.

Stone eventually hit upon a remarkably simple idea. He had thousands of bronze coins created that had three short words deeply engraved on each side: "DO IT NOW." He trained his salespeople to carry the coin in their pockets at all times, and to reach into their pocket and feel the writing on the coin whenever they felt themselves wavering about making a sales call or contacting a prospect.

It worked. The encouragement provided by that small coin was often all it took to defeat the enemy of procrastination.

Procrastination is not solved that easily in most life decisions. A recent *New York Times* article about procrastination sheds some light on the reasons and also alludes to some important biblical principles.[1]

The key point of the article is that procrastination is not basically about laziness or self-control. People engage in this irrational cycle of chronic procrastination because of an inability to manage negative moods around a task.

Procrastination is a problem of emotional regulation, not a time management problem. We get a momentary reward/relief from procrastinating, but procrastination only serves to exacerbate stress and distress.

To rewire any habit, we have to give our brains a better reward. Two key rewards, according to the article, are:

- Self-forgiveness
- Self-compassion

The article indirectly and unintentionally focuses the reader on a key biblical teaching. Jesus tells us in Mark 12:31 that the second great commandment is to "love your neighbor as yourself." That means we must be able to forgive ourselves (avoid shame) and have compassion (including love for ourselves).

At its core, as with many other bad habits and sins, procrastination is listening to the evil one and believing a lie: that we'll feel better if we put doing something off until later. The way to overcome that lie is to listen to the Holy Spirit.

Your Time to Decide

What possible reasons might you have for not beginning *now* to incorporate into your life the powerful principle of Sabbath?

_____

_____

_____

"Okay, Robert," you may be thinking, "I'm convinced. I want to start honoring the Sabbath. What now? What do I do with myself on my chosen Sabbath day?" The answer to that question is never the same for any two individuals, but there are some general truisms and principles, which we have already covered to some degree, that we should review.

Strategies for Four-Tank Sabbath Renewal

Let me start by reminding you that your objective in the Sabbath is rest. Not excitement. Not entertainment. And certainly not productivity. It may seem boring. Boredom is actually a feature of Sabbath rest, but it will take some time to break your addiction to busyness and become comfortable with the slow, still environment that leads to renewal.

Your strategy for enjoying and benefiting from this day of rest begins with understanding that you need to refill *all four* of your tanks—the physical, the mental, the emotional, and the spiritual.

I mentioned some of the ways I refill my mental, emotional, and physical tanks. We discussed this some in Chapters 3 and 7. What are two or three things that you will use to refill your:

Mental tank?

_____

_____

_____

_____

Emotional tank?

_____

_____

_____

_____

Physical tank?

_____

_____

_____

_____

What are some of the challenges or concerns that you have regarding your ability to keep these tanks full? Explain.

_____

_____

_____

_____

My near-death experience in the spring of 2018 brought home to me in the most vivid terms how wonderful it is to be alive.

Have you had a similar experience or known someone who has? Describe that experience.

_____

_____

_____

_____

Read 1 Timothy 6:17. Write down some things for which you have to be thankful.

_____

_____

_____

_____

Filling Your Most Important Tank

Besides scheduling a brief quiet time each day, it is vital to designate significant space in your day of rest for engaging with God. But what does that look like in practical terms? Here, in closing, allow me to share four steps the Lord has used powerfully and consistently in my Sabbath time with Him.

1. Quiet your mind. (Shut out all voices but God's.)

If you could see it, what would most people's souls look like all day long due to the competing thoughts and voices shouting for attention?

_____

_____

_____

_____

What negative emotions do you deal with the most?

_____

_____

_____

In Psalm 62, verses 1 and 5, and Psalm 42, what does David order his soul to do? How should it "behave"?

_____

_____

_____

What metaphor does David employ for his calmed soul in Psalm 131:2?

_____

_____

_____

What would it look like for you to "climb up in your heavenly Father's lap and be still"? How do you think it would feel?

_____

_____

_____

_____

2. Focus your mind. (Turn to God.)

Have you ever tried to think about nothing? It's not possible. You can't simply make your mind blank. So, once you've quieted your soul, it's vital to focus on something. Obviously, when your goal is to engage God, you must turn your focus toward Him.

Have you ever had the kind of critical, unfocused experience that I had in the story I related when I was a guest minister? What were the circumstances? What were the results?

_____

_____

_____

What does God hear when a person sings praises to Him? What kind of communication does God prefer to hear?

_____

_____

_____

According to Psalm 100:1–5, what is a perfect way to approach God?

_____

_____

_____

Have you ever heard a song on the radio or in a worship service and had the tune or lyrics come back into your mind throughout the day? What songs might God likely put into your heart as keys to His presence?

_____

_____

_____

You can sing the song out loud if you want to, but you don't have to. What's important is that you're focusing on Him. Singing to the Lord with thanksgiving turns your focus toward God. Music and worship represent a key element of your resting time with the Lord.

3. Pray your mind. (Talk to God.)

This next step is very simple. Just talk to God like you talk to anyone else. He is a person. He has a personality.

How were you taught to pray? Do you tend to pray or talk to God in ritualistic terms or very conversationally?

_____

_____

_____

_____

What kinds of things should and can we talk to God about?

_____

_____

_____

_____

List a few things that burden you and would be at the top of your mind to talk with God about right now.

_____

_____

_____

_____

What particular lie—based on religious-sounding terms—does Satan use to try to convince you that your prayers are not acceptable?

_____

_____

_____

_____

Philippians 4:6 says, "Be anxious for nothing. In everything by prayer and supplication let your requests be made known to God. And the peace of God, which surpasses all understanding, will guard your heart and mind through Christ Jesus."

In your own words, describe what your response will be to the enemy when he tries to convince you that your personal prayers are selfish.

_____

_____

_____

_____

4. Renew your mind. (Let God talk to you.)

I beseech you therefore, brethren, by the mercies of God, that you present your bodies a living sacrifice, holy, acceptable to God, which is your reasonable service. And do not be conformed to this world, but be transformed by the renewing of your mind, that you may prove what is that good and acceptable and perfect will of God. (Romans 12:1–2)

Respond to this statement: Renewing your mind—that is, replacing falsehood and deception with spiritual truth—changes you from the inside out.

_____

_____

_____

What are some of the ways God speaks to us?

_____

_____

_____

What is the most fundamental and sure way that God speaks to us?

_____

_____

_____

How did God's leading me to Genesis 35 and Deuteronomy 11, along with Genesis 28:7, open up my eyes and help unfold His leading me to plant Gateway Church?

_____

_____

_____

_____

God wants to speak with you. According to John 16:13–14, what kinds of things does God want to communicate to us through His Holy Spirit?

_____

_____

_____

_____

Would you like to be steered into truth rather than believing lies or being deceived? Wouldn't you like to know what's ahead so you can pray, prepare, and plan accordingly? Don't you want to know God's will for your life? Of course, your answer is yes to all of this. Well, the Spirit of God is ready, willing, and more than able to fulfill His mission in your life. The only barrier is our busyness and the noise with which we constantly surround ourselves. It's not that God isn't speaking; it's that we can't hear Him above the roar of our crazy, hurried lives.

Summarize the benefits and the power of taking a true day of Sabbath rest each week.

_____

_____

_____

_____

RSVP

Read Matthew 11:28–30 in The Message.
Respond to the image of Jesus as:
The Vine

_____

_____

_____

The Great Shepherd

_____
_____
_____
_____

The Great High Priest
_____
_____
_____

The Living Water
_____
_____
_____

The Warrior-King
_____
_____
_____

What were the excuses used by two of Jesus' hearers when He asked them to follow Him? What happened when they made the decision to attend to those things? Were those things really important? Why or why not?

_____
_____
_____
_____

The secret to living the Christian life joyfully, abundantly, peacefully, powerfully, and fruitfully is a shockingly simple one: put God first. I promise you—more importantly, God's Word promises you—everything else takes care of itself when you do. Put Him first in your relationships, first in your finances, and first in your time.

Will you accept God's invitation and put Him first in everything in your life, including your time? Will you *do it now*?

_____

_____

_____

_____

Key Quotes:

"Those who honor the principle of the Sabbath find the wind of heaven at their backs."

"It is vital to designate significant space in your day of rest for engaging with God."

"How do you enter God's presence? With singing!"

"Just talk to God like you talk to anyone else. He is a person. He has a personality."

"God wants to speak to you—clearly and powerfully. In fact, hearing what God has to say to you is the key to change and growth."

"The secret to living the Christian life joyfully, abundantly, peacefully, powerfully, and fruitfully is a shockingly simple one: put God first."

NOTES

Chapter 1

1. The Ten Commandments

Chapter 2

1. Npr.org, *The Two-Way*, March 1, 2018. Accessed July 20, 2019. https://www.npr.org /sections/thetwo-way/2018/03/01/589895641/south-korea-shortens-inhumanely -long-work-week.
2. Massachusetts government online. Accessed July 21, 2019. https://www.mass.gov /guides/breaks-and-time-off#-day-of-rest.
3. Saima Salim, Digital Information World, January 4, 2019.
4. Stephen R. Covey, A. Roger Merrill, and Rebecca R. Merrill, *First Things First* (New York: Free Press, 1994), 88.

Chapter 3

1. Saundra Dalton-Smith, *Sacred Rest: Recover Your Life, Renew Your Energy, Restore Your Sanity* (New York: FaithWords, 2017), 41.
2. Linda Malone, *Everyday Health*, April 16, 2015. "10 Brain Exercises That Boost Memory." Accessed July 20, 2019. https://www.everydayhealth.com/longevity/mental -fitness/brain-exercises-for-memory.aspx.

Chapter 4

1. https://www2.kenyon.edu/Depts/Religion/Projects/Reln91/Blood/Judaism /kashrut/kashrut.htm
2. Mark Buchanan, *The Rest of God: Restoring Your Soul by Restoring Sabbath*, Kindle ed. (repr., Nashville, Tennessee: Thomas Nelson, 2006), 106–107.

Chapter 5

1. Grace Donnelly, "Here's Why Life Expectancy in the U.S. Dropped Again This Year," *Fortune*, 2018, http://fortune.com/2018/02/09/us-life-expectancy-dropped-again/.
2. Steven H. Woolf and Laudan Aron, "Failing Health of the United States," BMJ.com, 2018, https://www.bmj.com/content/360/bmj.k496.
3. Abby Haglage, "U.S. Life Expectancy Has Fallen Again. Here Are Three Reasons Why," Yahoo, 2018, https://sg.news.yahoo.com/u-s-life-expectancy-keeps-dropping-alcohol-blame-185004863.html.
4. Tracey R. Rich, "Judaism 101: Shabbat," Jewfaq.org. Accessed June 25, 2019, http://www.jewfaq.org/shabbat.htm.

Chapter 6

1. Fran Howarth, "The Perils of Unused Vacation Time," Spark, 2018, https://www.adp.com/spark/articles/2018/07/the-perils-of-unused-vacation-time.aspx.
2. "Under-Vacationed America: A State-by-State Look at Time Off," U.S. Travel Association, 2018, https://www.ustravel.org/research/under-vacationed-america-state-state-look-time.

Chapter 10

1. Charlotte Lieberman, "Why You Procrastinate (It Has Nothing to Do with Self-Control)," *New York Times*, March 25, 2019, https://www.nytimes.com/2019/03/25/smarter-living/why-you-procrastinate-it-has-nothing-to-do-with-self-control.html.

ABOUT THE AUTHOR

ROBERT MORRIS is the founding lead senior pastor of Gateway Church, a multicampus church based out of the Dallas–Fort Worth metroplex. Since it began in 2000, the church has grown to more than 71,000 active attendees. His television program is aired in over 190 countries, and his radio program, *Worship & the Word with Pastor Robert*, airs in more than 1,800 radio markets across America. He serves as chancellor of The King's University and is the bestselling author of numerous books, including *The Blessed Life*, *Frequency*, *Beyond Blessed*, and *Take the Day Off*. Robert and his wife, Debbie, have been married thirty-nine years and are blessed with one married daughter, two married sons, and nine grandchildren.